The
ALL-*for*-NOTHING
MARRIAGE

4 Steps to a Meaningful Marriage

Daniel Zopoula

 FriesenPress

Suite 300 - 990 Fort St
Victoria, BC, V8V 3K2
Canada

www.friesenpress.com

ISBN
978-1-5255-5222-9 (Hardcover)
978-1-5255-5223-6 (Paperback)
978-1-5255-5224-3 (eBook)

1. Family & Relationships, Marriage

Distributed to the trade by The Ingram Book Company

Table of Contents

Praise for
The All -*for*- Nothing Marriage

"No problem is more urgent today than developing strong marriages. Bishop Daniel Zopoula has written a book with important insights that can help strengthen any marriage. I highly recommend his approach and development of this topic. You will find new and important understandings in this book."

   Archbishop Robert L. Wise, author of When There Is No Miracle

"I love this book! Daniel has laid out a very practical, step by step plan for the revitalization of a marriage that has drifted into mediocrity. I appreciate that he uses his own marriage challenges as the motivation for finding down-to-earth solutions for developing and maintaining healthy marriages for others.

"As a psychologist for over 38 years, Sherry and I have done our share of marriage counselling so I appreciated Daniel's emphasis on the Biblical concept of "agape love" as the foundation of his discussion. As Daniel stated, 'The gift of love has no entitlements, insurances or guarantees.' He wisely counsels the reader to 'outsource your need to God, your higher power.' I also found this next statement very helpful: 'Your challenge is not to find the right person to love; it's to love the person you find.'

"His discussion of 'closeness' and 'flexibility' was very helpful. Too much of either is a disaster waiting to happen in the marriage. As

Daniel stated, couples need a balance of 'we' and 'I'. I particularly liked Chapter 8 'The Compatibility Myth'. Too many marriages move toward divorce because they feel they have lost their compatibility. I believe, as does Daniel, that differences are designed by God to challenge us to make healthy changes in our own personality characteristics, not changes in our spouse's.

"I found Daniel to be very honest in his discussion of marriage. He states that marriage is a life-long journey of change. As you read this book, you will see that Daniel's focus is changing yourself not your spouse. In the marriage counselling that we do our first rule is: 'You can't change your spouse; you can only change yourself. So, what are you willing to change?' Daniel's insights into marriage conflict, and the six common marriage conflicts, was full of practical wisdom. Well done, Daniel!

"I appreciate his continual focus on love as the most powerful force on earth to change lives, to change marriages and to change the world. Keep preaching this truth, Daniel. I was personally motivated by Lesson 2 on prioritizing your marriage. In the midst of helping many other marriages, I realize that sometimes my own marriage growth takes a back seat to the needs of many other marriages. Good check for me!

"I also like that Daniel has developed a 4-Step Plan to give some practical application to what he has written about in Part 1. In Steps 1 and 2 he gives excellent advice and practical direction to give hands-on help to what it means to love your spouse. Daniel does much the same thing in Step 3, Choose a Winning Attitude. He challenges our current thinking about marital relationships and encourages new perspectives on life and marriage. Some excellent thought-provoking wisdom in this section. In Step 4, Daniel tells us that all the advice in the world will not help us if we do not apply this wisdom with all our hearts.

"All marriages need continual upgrading so they aren't taken for granted and then fall into survival mode. Daniel has provided a practical guide for this purpose but has also delivered some good motivation for marriage growth through his teaching on 'agape' love."

Graham Bretherick, Chartered Psychologist
author of Healing Life's Hurts

To my Beloved, Sara, my wife of noble character, thank you. The struggle is real, but you just won't give up on this bushman! Without your friendship and encouragement, much of the work on which this book is based might well have remained undone. To my daughters, Affia, Dansia, and my son, Daniel Jr. Thank you for your generosity and the patience you manifested even when you had to endure your mother reading each word of this book to you in the van as we traveled from place to place.

To Dr. Cassidy Klima, a valued friend who's expertise in scientific communication aided in editing and paring down much of the content that eventually made its way into this document- many, many thanks!

To Rev. Joel Klemick, a gifted writer and a treasured brother who knows when I need consolation and when I need a challenge. Many thanks for your valuable contribution, together with Rev. Frank and Jessica Allen, who stood with me, unfeignedly.

To Graham Bretherick, Anthony & Sonya White, Doug & Marsha Graveland, Jim & Mary Gail Lietch, Mary-Jean Klima, Wes Mills, Sammy and Kristen Golom, Shawn and Tina Mehler, Dr. Ken Keis, Dr. Travis,+ Todd Atkinson, Peter & Deborah Struck, + Ed Gungor, Sara Bieniada, Rick & Ruth Melvin, Richard & Joanna Zazula. You gave various versions of this manuscript a thoughtful reading, and I am grateful for your gracious reviews and encouragements. Your confidence and companionship mean a great deal to me.

INTRODUCTION

RECENTLY, A YOUNG man I know well proposed to a beautiful young woman in the most romantic of ways. He set up a walk in the woods near the home of her youth, an exercise that required several hours of driving. Friends who'd been drafted into the adventure went ahead to a clearing and laid out a blanket with candles. He had photographers on hand to capture her joyful response as he knelt, offered the ring, and asked the question. It worked. She was overcome with emotion and her "yes" was one of full desire and commitment. After a brief engagement, I officiated their ceremony and sent them into their life together.

Their engagement story is like many others, like many of yours who are reading this now. A special moment, a careful proposal, and a hearty "Yes!" It was a moment of joy-filled bliss, brimming with hopeful anticipation of the life they would build together. A life built on dreams of love and intimacy of the kind fairytales are made. But in actuality, it is also a moment of profound ignorance.

We all have a story about how we fell in love. Do you remember yours? It's no secret that many of us have a story about how we fell *out* of love, too. For some couples, the impetus was financial stress, a challenging child, the loss of a loved one, an affair, an addiction, an accident, an illness, an obsession, or unresolved issues from the past.

Truthfully, for every two marriages that grow from such a proposal story, one will end in divorce. Each of those beginnings is shaped by confidence that they have found "the one"—that other person so uniquely designed for them that they quote *Jerry Maguire*, passionately saying, "You complete me!"

All couples begin with dreams of a marriage with such interconnection that there is no dissuading them in those early days. Nor should there be. However, going forward, if they remain ignorant, they will be blind to all the invisible forces that bear down on their relationship. These forces conspire to first strain and weaken, and then to eventually cause unmatched pain and heartache. This can lead to seemingly irreversible emotional separation, in which permanent separation—divorce—seems the only way out.

Of course, divorce is no easy solution. It can lead to unimaginable financial complexity, and unresolved bitterness. It creates divided loyalties in the relationships that once enhanced life together. Should there be kids involved, fierce competition can emerge over the best fruit from a marriage that began with such good intentions. In this way, divorce is one ditch on the path of marriage.

On the other side of the road, however, there is another ditch that can be equally painful. This ditch holds a loveless, disconnected, depressing living arrangement that began as a marriage. While some married couples call it quits, others settle for being roommates. In doing so, they adopt a relationship of apparent convenience, filled with misery while facilitating co-parenting, cohabiting, and other shared expenses. But like divorce, staying together in this fashion comes at tremendous unseen costs.

Each ditch—divorce on one side, a loveless and hopeless marriage on the other—comes at the cost of the life imagined on that day one partner first slid a ring over the finger of another. Dreams die a slow and violent death in our hearts. A death that takes a piece of our own life with it and leaves in its place despair, discouragement, depression, and destruction.

Perhaps that is why, as divorce rates continue to climb, each successive generation is less likely to marry than the one before. It seems an attempt to escape the perceived harm of failed marriages. But while the relationship they have may not be called "marriage" by name, it bears all the same marks and effects, and the eventual decline and separation carry the same difficulties.

Divorce does not favour socio-economic classes, religions, ethnicities, or political leanings. It comes for all of us equally. And it brings with it a destruction and complexity that leaks into all other relationships, life aspirations, and the very idea of who you are. Second and third marriages are more precarious than first ones. If you think you are exempt, you might be right. And you might not be. If you have children, the chances are it will be one of them.

But it need not be so. You see, marriage itself is not the problem. And most often, neither are the individual parties that make up the marriage—the spouse, the life partner. Rather, it is the accumulated set of unreasonable demands, expectations, and ways of relating that we import to the relationship that slowly, moment by moment and day by day, tear apart the bond we vow to uphold.

I believe that everyone is entitled to a meaningful marriage filled with passion, intimacy, and shared purpose. And it is my goal to help anyone achieve this through *The All-for-Nothing Marriage*. With this program, you will learn step-by-step strategies to neutralize your problems through the adoption of a new and redemptive mindset, one that will shift the momentum of your marriage for good. The program can work for any couple—anyone can easily stop disappointment, eliminate silent frustrations, and build a meaningful relationship by using the *series of disciplines taught here. The tools and skills you develop will allow you to create unity—*an *emotional togetherness* that magically turns mediocre marriages into remarkable ones. Marriage is a sacred space in which you are both meant to be fully realized. So, let's make sure you are set up to succeed in achieving and maintaining that phenomenal marriage you and your partner envision for your future.

NOTES & PERSONAL JOURNAL PAGE

Why Another Book on Marriage?

WHEN IT COMES to books on marriage, we are spoiled for choices. With so many on the market, I second-guessed myself about committing these words to the page. Aren't there enough books written on the topic already? Am I wasting my time and that of my readers? Would one more reasonable person be willing to invest in another marriage program to achieve their goals?

Further, I subscribe to the concepts I've described here personally and so was self-conscious about putting myself out there. I became concerned with what others would think. What if people rejected and condemned what I had to say? Surely that would put my humble person under increased scrutiny and attention!

I am embarrassed to say that this self-doubt almost caused me to cancel this book. They say that private victory is the victory over self. I cannot hope to lead others until I can lead my own life with integrity and manage myself with discipline. So, I examined my motives and this is the conclusion I came to.

With this book, I want to contribute meaningfully of myself in a way that will produce success for others in their relationships.

As you go through these pages, it will become clear that the perspectives I try to help build have come from my own research and experiences. And, based on my own successes and failures, I can personally endorse that the topics this book covers provide a practical tool for creating that core connection that results in phenomenal love and ultimate life fulfillment.

So, this book is a means for me to steward my unique contribution—a way for me to share my knowledge and experience with you, unapologetically and unashamedly, regardless of material rewards or circumstances. It is a statement about my lack of concern over whether other people have already written and are selling great books on marriage.

I have brought what lessons the Lord has blessed me with along my journey. I am turning them over to you. And I hope that what fruit comes to your relationship, from the sessions I guide you through, will be blessed in multitude.

NOTES & PERSONAL JOURNAL PAGE

_____

_____

_____

_____

_____

_____

_____

_____

_____

_____

_____

_____

_____

Defining Marriage

IN MOST CASES, with the exception of the religious and legal dimension, most couples are already married on some level before their wedding day. The movement toward marriage generally begins privately, driven by attracting forces that draw the couple together. This leads to a verbal/nonverbal indication of commitment, and then is followed by a public declaration of intention. As a result, by the time the ceremony arrives, the relationship is often already operational on many levels: socially, geographically, sexually, emotionally, intellectually, and economically. The wedding ceremony often acknowledges what has already taken place on a more private and psychological plane.

So, what does it mean to be married? Marriage has widely diverse meanings amongst all people. There is no one definition of marriage that provides it complete legitimacy or encompasses all its dimensions. Philosophers wrestle with defining it, sociologists struggle to measure it, and psychologists try to describe it. Therefore, *no matter how thoroughly marriage is examined, it maintains a sacred mystery that likely defies it from a total explanation. However, we must define marriage and its architecture if we are to have any meaningful discussions surrounding it.*

It is my belief that *marriage is a sacred space—a blame-free zone—where you give yourself completely and intimately to another.* In marriage, you can feel more visible and valued. Your life becomes fully available to self and to your spouse. Here, you can become your fullest, most yielded and most formed, to the delight of God. In this soulful space, you intentionally receive reality, including your own, as divine—to be honoured but never defiled. This definition presumes ontological equality and functional subordination. Those sound like complicated terms, but they are actually simple when defined. *Ontological equality means that man and woman are equal in the eyes of God and in the eyes of the law. Functional subordination means that in all things, all matters, responsibilities are shared. Duties are shared according to gifting, strengths, and abilities.*

In many Christian subcultures, the man is seen as the head of the home. This can be a divisive and provocative concept, but it needn't be if understood correctly through ontological equality and functional subordination. *The concept of "headship of the home" speaks to the symbol of the presence of Christ in His church. Notwithstanding this lofty and esteemed position, Christ served his disciples. He served the church. He washed the feet of His disciples. He took the place of the servant, to the point that He laid down His own life for others. This,* He said, is the greatest act of love. This means that man is to model service in the home. Not only that, but to model the spirit in which to serve: Joyful service. This is a leadership in being ready to serve first, not be served. *So, when it comes to the essence of being, man and woman are equal. When it comes to functional responsibilities, man and woman mutually submit to one another.* This is what it means to be married!

NOTES & PERSONAL JOURNAL PAGE

Origin of the All-for-Nothing Marriage

THE CONCEPT FOR the All-for-Nothing Marriage began at the heart of my own life experience. My wife and I are in a cross-cultural marriage. And like many, we eventually found ourselves in a space where we were trying desperately to solve our marital problems. We were very frustrated with each other. But the harder we tried to solve things, the more stressed out we felt. Every time we talked about a problem, we not only failed to resolve it but ended up fighting and making matters worse. Rather than being a source of joy, our marriage started to erode the quality of our lives.

I became so sick and tired of the emotional pain, sleepless nights, and tension that, in frustration one night, I purchased every decent book I could find on marriage. (Unbeknownst to me, my wife was doing the same thing!) I pored through these volumes, and although I did receive some interesting tips and heard some helpful, probing questions, *I discovered that all of these resources had the same fatal flaw:* **They operated within pathological frameworks.** The majority of these relationship books employed traditional clinical approaches that focus on **problem-solving strategies** and **communication skills**, with high emphasis on partners' **temperaments** and **compatibility**.

I had just experienced firsthand that obsessing about solving marriage problems *stressed my relationship out further and made my problems worse.* I thought: How crazy is it that so few ever write about this issue?

So, I went back to my Bible and began reading Paul's Letters to the Corinthians. I read and re-read the love chapters. **And then a couple of things dawned on me. First: The mother of all problems in marriage manifests as defective connection lines between spouses. And, second: Ultimately, love is the only answer to this issue.** Love alone is the dominant force in the universe. It determines the experience of your life.

The Greeks had three ways to describe the varied manifestations of the reality of love. **Eros** describes romantic love, **philia** describes companionship or friendship, and **agape** describes a love of giving oneself away freely, no less for the villain than for the victim. The definition of "agape" caught me off guard. *Here we are talking about unconditional love—the kind that is not given in order to get.* I realized right then that something about the way I viewed marriage and my role in it had to change.

So, I developed a course called "**100-to-None** Marriages." Then, as more and more people asked for guidance, I designed the *All-for-Nothing Marriage* booklet as an **experimental thought.** With its success, I have finally written the full concept down here to share more widely.

I didn't set out to become an expert on how the best marriages work. I was in a pickle, and I had to learn how to get my marriage to work for the common good. *I had to learn how to manage disappointment, eliminate silent frustrations, and get the marriage I really wanted.* Through this process, I was motivated to learn for myself. And I did, with great success!

What you can expect from this book is a straightforward do-it-yourself plan to help you achieve a meaningful marriage. *The course will provide tools that can help you keep your connection strong and re-establish those ties when they are threatened by the seasons of marriage that roll through. As you read along, you will experience a shift in your ideas about love and commitment. You'll understand the dynamics of marriage like never before. You'll gain amazing insights into the inner workings of primary love and a corresponding system I call* The All-*for*-Nothing Marriage Method. *I will walk you through the process as I explain the philosophy underlying my unique take on today's marriage solutions.*

The process for this journey is simple. The All-*for*-Nothing Marriage **Book** is broken up into various chapters, each addressing one of the major conversations you and your spouse can have. Unlike traditional marital counselling curriculums, *The All-for-Nothing Marriage* is not a compatibility exercise. Its goal is to create a paradigm shift, not to determine suitability or compatibility. This isn't a list of do's and don'ts, or right or wrong conversations, but a way to understand one another better.

Although *The* All-*for*-Nothing *Marriage Method* is a tool designed for those preparing to marry, if you've already made the leap into marriage and are looking for something like marital counselling, **you'll get just as much out of this course as anybody looking to make their vows.** Your children, grandchildren, and great grandchildren will all benefit from the heart-to-heart conversations you're about to have with each other. Your marriage may be saved because of the journey on which you're about to embark.

I wish my wife and I had this course before we got married. It would have saved us from much struggle. Thankfully, we were able to find help through a great friend, a man full of wisdom and grace. I discuss much of what he helped us learn about connecting at our cores, shifting our focus from demanding character change, and leaving behind dealing with our problems, and starting to becoming soulmates at length through this course. I am going to encourage you to have many of the critical conversations he encouraged my wife and I to have, about our families of origin, the critical scenes that shaped us, our personality styles and the way we process emotions. I am confident that working through this space will likewise set you and your partner up for a beautiful and successful marriage that is free of major drama and filled with joy.

NOTES & PERSONAL JOURNAL PAGE

PART 1:

THE ANATOMY OF A MEANINGFUL MARRIAGE

Summary

PART ONE OF this book looks into the structures and internal workings of marriage: What is the nature of marriage? This section lays the foundation for understanding the dimensions of marriage and what motivates it, its key requirements, myths about compatibility, and common problems that can hinder healthy connection with your partner.

Part Two provides a strategy called "The All-*for*-Nothing Marriage Four-Step Plan" as a tool to enhance your marriage. Part Two will challenge you to develop positive attitudes and actions that will greatly enhance the climate of your marriage. This section will give you practical ideas for rekindling your marriage. In other words, Part One lays the philosophy, and Part Two gives a plan for its implementation.

NOTES & PERSONAL JOURNAL PAGE

_____

_____

_____

_____

_____

_____

_____

_____

_____

_____

_____

_____

_____

_____

Lesson 1: Sometimes, The Map Is Wrong

IN HIS BOOK, *Too Soon Old, Too Late Smart,* Gordon Livingston tells a story of a young lieutenant in the 82nd Airborne Division who is trying to orient himself in the field at Fort Bragg, North Carolina. As he stood studying a map, his platoon sergeant approached. "You figure out where we are, lieutenant?" the sergeant asked.

"Well, the map says there should be a hill over there, but I don't see it," the lieutenant replied.

"Sir," the platoon sergeant said, "if the map don't agree with the ground, then the map is wrong."

What a profound truth!

Concerning relationships, our journeys through life consist of an effort to conform our "mental maps" to the ground on which we walk. Yet, our "mental maps" become faulty when based on the flawed concept of romantic love. Romantic love is an earthly paradise (or shared delusion) that influences our choice in partners. This state can be based in many things but typically prioritizes what we think makes us compatible: sexual attraction, education, earning potential, shared interests, and trustworthiness. When these conditions are not fully realized or maintained, relationships dissolve.

For most couples, the "maps" in their heads don't agree with the ground on which they walk. Their fantasies set them up for disappointment. They become disoriented or lost and forget where they are going. They lose identity and become incapable of making a unique contribution to the relationship.

If you had an inaccurate map of a city, and you were looking for a certain location, you would become both lost and frustrated. If someone counselled you to try harder, and you doubled your speed, you would merely be lost twice as fast. If the person sensed how discouraged you were and counselled you to think positively rather than negatively, you would still be lost—but perhaps you wouldn't care about it as much. At this point in your journey, your lack of progress, your "doing nothing," may have produced frustration and discouragement. It could appear superficially that the problem is laziness, or a negative approach. But the problem would have nothing to do with either diligence or attitude. The real problem would be an inaccurate map.

Over many years, I have listened to many, many people's stories. I have heard all the ways that things can go awry in marriages. It is the accumulated set of unreasonable demands, expectations, and ways of relating that we import to the relationship that slowly, moment by moment and day by day, tear apart the bond we vow to uphold. In our marriages, our faulty maps lead us into ditches. Divorce on one side, or potentially staying together in misery on the other. Like Livingston, I too have learned that our passage through life consists of an effort to get the maps in our heads to conform to the ground on which we walk. The requirement for a hope-filled and fulfilling marriage then, is a reliable navigation system that can correct our course.

That is the aim of this course: designing and implementing better maps. The "mental map" we construct in our heads must serve to allow us to align ourselves to get where we wish to go: a meaningful marriage in the context of a well-connected life and a lifestyle that can bear up under the weight of our anxiety driven lives. Then we will manifest as authentic and powerful expressions of God's purpose and presence.

While there are dangerous ditches on either side of the road, there remains a wide, tested, strong road on which it is safe to travel. There remain obstacles on the road, but those obstacles offer opportunity through which to strengthen our bonds, not be divided by them.

NOTES & PERSONAL JOURNAL PAGE

_____

_____

_____

_____

_____

_____

_____

_____

_____

_____

_____

_____

_____

_____

Lesson 2: The Key to a Phenomenal Marriage

CORRECT MAPS WILL impact our effectiveness. It is imperative to get the maps in our heads to conform to the ground on which we walk. However, when the territory is constantly changing, any map is soon obsolete. Inaccurate maps are a source of frustration for couples who are trying to find their way to meaningful relationships. What's needed is a moral compass. The compass orients people to the desired coordinates and provides a path forward even in hostile and unsettled terrain. For the purposes of this book, we would describe primary love as that compass.

As I said earlier, I restate that, broadly used, love describes an emotional attraction between two or more people. The Greeks had three kinds of love to describe the varied manifestations of this single reality of love. **Eros** describes the love between lovers, **philia** describes companionship or friendship, and **agape** describes a love of *giving oneself away freely, no less for the villain than for the victim.* In other words, **agape** love is an "**All**-*for*-**Nothing**" proposition. *It is unconditional. It is not given in order to get.*

With agape, you do not need to feel loved to give. In the Christian sense, love is not primarily an emotion, but an act of the **yielded** will. At times, feelings of love can follow after agape. Thus, in agape's terms, we can love all persons without necessarily liking them. **In fact, liking them may stand in the way of loving** them, by making us overprotective and lovey-dovey instead of reasonably honest friends.

Agape can be a powerful tool in a marriage to rekindle feelings of affection and love when they have waned. Agape can also be extended to family members and friends to develop, enhance, or maintain relationships. Using this principle, it is possible to actively create connection, strengthen the relationship, and renew feelings of commitment.

It is important that we be guided by agape love, so that we adhere to the internal compass that will lead us to the strong and fulfilling marriage we're building. This way, when romantic love—or **Eros**—wanes, we can still love with complete devotion. When friendship—or **philia**—is strained, we are still united in a shared vision and direction.

For the rest of this book, we will identify **primary love** as a form of agape love, and define it as the *giving of oneself away freely, irrespective of the worthiness of the recipient.* Sections of this book will offer more insight into the inner-workings of primary love and a system for its application, called *The All-for-Nothing Marriage Method.*

NOTES & PERSONAL JOURNAL PAGE

Lesson 3: Hundred to None

NOW THAT WE understand the nature of agape love, we are able to say goodbye to the proportionality of contribution that sees marriage as a fifty-fifty requirement. That is, that your marriage is a culmination of contribution that is half yours and half your partner's. Agape love destroys that notion. Agape love is a 100-to-none concept. In practical terms, this means I come to my marriage ready to give everything, 100 percent, and to demand nothing in return.

Through this, every action you undertake in your marriage is ideally an unconditional gift. In agape, love is a gift, sex is a gift, service is a gift. These are not business transactions in which doing something earns you merit. The gift of love has no entitlements, insurances, or guarantees. In 100-to-none, you serve joyfully. You do all things joyfully or you don't do them at all. This kind of giving is redemptive. These refined, yielded gifts are surrendered to God first, and human second.

In this paradigm, there is a shift in focus. The expectation is no longer placed on your partner but on yourself. In this space, you gain freedom through control of "self." In truth, we have no ability to control "else" and the struggle to manipulate the reactions and behaviours of another often leads to misery. Harnessing the control of one's "self" leads to freedom from the slavery of manipulative behaviours and the associated frustration and disappointment in not achieving the desired outcomes. If you are free from expectation of "else," you experience less misunderstanding because you are seeking to understand rather than to be understood. You eliminate silent frustration due to unspoken expectation, and you get the marriage you really want.

This 100-to-none is not accomplishable on your own, but through divine grace. When the gift is given to God first, it frees the giver from any expectation of the receiver. The offering is done primarily unto God. This also frees the receiver from any expectation. If you give this way, there is blessing, because God is the source of blessing and it is He who gives the fruit. Give and you shall receive (Jesus, Luke 6:38). But receive from whom? From God—not humans. Whatever you give in such a way to your partner, no matter how unimportant it seemed, you did for the Lord.

So, marriage is a 100-to-none, and it provides no guarantee. That's right. Your partner may not always treat you well. Some people are toxic. They are so wounded that they destroy other people, they take their spouse for granted, and they do not respect their spouse's reality. I cannot reach them. I can only reach you. So, let me tell it to you plainly: No relationship has a right to destroy those parts of yourself that you bring to it: Your selfhood, your humanness, your vows, your faith—these are sacred. Those are the foundation you bring to the marriage. They are the realm of the divine. You have no right to let your partner destroy you.

NOTES & PERSONAL JOURNAL PAGE

_____

_____

_____

_____

_____

_____

_____

_____

_____

_____

_____

_____

Lesson 4: Motivation for Marriage

ONE MOTIVATING FACTOR for marriage is the fulfillment of needs. **It is admirable to say that we are marrying someone to help them fulfill their needs. But the truth is that we hope and believe our needs will be met too.**

Most couples choose each other based on the potential that they will receive a sense of worth and well-being from their partner. It is as if many individuals view themselves as incomplete and a potential mate represents the possibility of psychological completion. **The desire for wholeness and completion then becomes a powerful force that creates bonding and dependency in the marital relationship.**

A psychologist named Abraham Maslow suggested that each person has certain basic needs in their life. He listed these needs in order of importance. First, a person seeks to fulfill their physiological needs. These are things that are necessary in order to sustain life: food, water, oxygen, rest, etc. Second, a person seeks to fulfill needs for safety, which include the need for a safe environment, protection from harm, etc. Third, a person seeks to fulfill their need for love and belonging. This includes a desire for affectionate relationships with others. Fourth, a person seeks to fulfill his or her need for esteem. Esteem involves receiving recognition as a worthwhile person. Fifth, after the other levels of needs are finally met, a person seeks to fulfill the need of self-actualization. This is the need to become the person one has the potential to become, to develop into a full, creative person.

In today's society we are asking more of our spouses than ever, perhaps even more than they can afford to offer! Our predecessors typically looked to their marriage to fulfill the first two levels of needs in each other—the physiological and safety needs. But these days, marriage has become a matter of getting our higher needs met—those of personal development, self-expression, and love.

However, meeting higher-level needs is only accomplished through God and our own making, not through the makings of others. Depending on others for this can produce an unhealthy dependency and an unmeetable expectation.

That isn't to say that our partners do not have an impact on how we experience love and a sense of belonging, or how we can shape our self-worth and personal awareness. In fact, they can be our best resources for our achievement of these needs—as cheerleaders, advocates, counselors, and commiserants. But ultimately our partners are not able to manifest these things for us the way we would like them to. It is unhealthy to make them accountable for an outcome that they cannot control: **wholeness and completion.**

This is a situation in which we are seeking to fill a legitimate need through illegitimate means. In these spaces, we will begin to find ourselves listless and dissatisfied with our relationship. Our connection will become strained, and eventually our marriage will head toward a ditch. **Couples who rely on others to fulfill them frequently set themselves up for frustration and less-than-optimal relationships. But this is not to say that healthy couples take each other for granted. They respect each other's needs for wholeness and completion, they support each other's personal formation, self-actualization, and love. Cultivating realistic expectations and understanding the mechanisms of a healthy relationship are key ingredients of a successful marriage.**

Do not expect your marriage to meet all of your needs for you, specifically those you can only meet yourself. Take control over meeting your own higher-level needs. Ultimately, outsource your need to God, your higher power.

This topic and some tools you can use to prevent expectation from sidelining your marriage will be addressed further in Part Two of this book.

If you're interested, psychologist Eli Finkel discusses various aspects of this argument in his book, *The All-or-Nothing Marriage: How the Best Marriages Work.*

NOTES & PERSONAL JOURNAL PAGE

Lesson 5: Personal Fulfilment and Marital Commitment

ONE OF THE cornerstones of a successful marriage is commitment, an unwavering devotion to a relationship and partner. People can marry for a variety of reasons. However, all people—regardless of gender, culture, or creed—marry in order to do something to, or for, themselves: live, love, grow, leave a legacy, and to take a journey toward a better future. **Some marry to get. Other people marry to give.**

People can become committed for moral, practical, or structural reasons, all of which keep a marriage intact. But these commitments are to the idea, not the person. **Couples who are committed out of moral reasons** typically subscribe to religious beliefs or social norms that compel them to stay in their marriage out of duty and obligation. **Structurally committed couples** believe they have no choice but to stay married, because their lives have become too entangled to go. Material possessions, children, and a social life together can make it inconvenient to leave a relationship.

While moral and structural commitments may keep a marriage intact, they don't affect how partners feel about each other. For both moral and structural commitment, external factors are required to keep the marriage together. Partners believe they have no choice but to stay married, regardless of whether they're happy. In the All-for-Nothing Model, commitment is gratuitous —the kind that is not given in order to get. The commitment is given joyfully and freely, powered by divine grace and benevolence.

As a result, All-for-Nothing committed partners see their relationship and emotional bond as the most important things in their lives. **They stay married because they choose to, not out of necessity or a sense of responsibility. They stay married out of a generosity that is God-breathed. They tend to sacrifice personal agendas to focus on those that serve their togetherness.**

They think of themselves not as individuals but as a team, sharing aspirations, thoughts, and interests, all of which strengthen their desire to stay together to the glory of God. The phonetic of the word "together" gives insight into its meaning: It is "to get there." In other words, it is "together" in order "to get there."

By this perspective, in the All-for-Nothing Marriage, the primary pursuit of personal fulfilment is incompatible with the pursuit of marital commitment. **There is an idea out there that the primary function of marriage is to promote the spouses' personal fulfilment, i.e., to maximize their pleasure-to-pain ratio.** This belief elevates happiness as the highest end for a marriage. But doing so is dangerous, as it comes with the intolerable position that a marriage ceases when happiness ceases.

Unfortunately, people are also taught that building a successful, long-lasting marriage is a central means to self-expression and a meaningful life. The consequence of this is the associated belief that sustaining a happy marriage should not require extensive endurance, sacrifice, or forbearance. Virtually all marriages go through extended seasons during which the pleasure-to-pain ratio is low. In fact, for many couples, it might sometimes seem that a different relationship would offer a more favourable ratio.

Consequently, as spouses undergo periods when the marriage is challenging or painful, divorce feels like a reasonable choice. In contrast, in the All-for-Nothing Marriage, **when spouses undergo difficult periods in the marriage, they perceive those spaces as opportunities for personal and relationship growth as a consequence of working through the challenges together, as soulmates.**

To learn more about the topic of this chapter, I recommend The All-or-Nothing Marriage: How the Best Marriages Work, by Eli J. Finkel. This is an excellent book that discusses comprehensively the happiness-based model, which I believe is both prevalent and harmful.

In the same way, I also recommend Robert F. Stahmann and William J. Hiebert's Premarital and Remarital Counseling: The Professional's Handbook.

NOTES & PERSONAL JOURNAL PAGE

Lesson 6: The Dimensions of Marriage

MARRIAGE FACILITATES TWO integral people coming together to create a meaningful social synergy. The notion of this coming-together highlights a central moral imperative: *Marriage must not dissolve each of the persons who create it.* Each person must retain their identity while drawing together in a meaningful relationship as a couple. In order to maintain personhood in this space, it is important to be aware of the forces that fuel connection and flexibility within family interactions. They can interfere with preserving self. In healthy relationships, individuals enjoy time together *and* time apart. This balance is an important aspect of closeness.

Closeness examines the balance of separateness and togetherness—the dependence and independence in a relationship. Couples who are too close may become too dependent and smother each other. Overly connected relationships have an extreme amount of closeness. Loyalty is demanded at all costs. They are too controlling and may become too imposing and domineering. These relationships focus too much on togetherness, or *"We."* In contrast, too little closeness may result in disengagement, emotional detachment, or unavailability. Disconnected relationships have an intense level of emotional separateness. Members of the family are emotionally absent and unavailable; they are too independent. This unbalance manifests when there is too much focus on the *"I."*

Flexibility examines how the family is governed. In overly flexible families, everything is permissible. Anarchy governs. Decision-making is impulsive, discipline is erratic, and nobody is in charge. In contrast, inflexible relationships are black-and-white environments. Choices are dictated by the needs of the husband, wife, or kids. Leadership is imposing and domineering. Discipline is strict. There is no freedom. The relationship is inflexible and unbending. Without personal choice and preference, a spouse can feel trapped and lost, family members can lose their voices. Rebellion seems the only way out of the inflexible environment that is created.

In order for relationships to thrive, couples need a balance of "We" and "I," a comfortable level of both emotional closeness and emotional separateness, control and freedom.

You adapted your personal style preference from your family of origin. In marrying another person, you marry their family. Families' marked differences in closeness and flexibility styles can present significant challenges for you as a couple.

To learn more about the topic of this chapter, I recommend D. H. Olson's "Circumplex Model of Marital and Family Systems" from the *Journal of Family Therapy, 22, 144-167* (2000). It's an excellent resource that discusses the subject at hand comprehensively.

I also recommend Robert F. Stahmann and William J. Hiebert's *Premarital and Remarital Counseling: The Professional's Handbook.* It is an excellent book that discusses the subject at hand; any marriage guide would find it very helpful.

NOTES & PERSONAL JOURNAL PAGE

_____

_____

_____

_____

_____

_____

_____

_____

_____

_____

_____

_____

_____

Lesson 7: Seasons of Marriage

MARRIAGES ARE PERPETUALLY in a state of transition. And just as nature sees us moving from seasons of plenty to seasons of scarcity, your marriage can move from seasons of connection to seasons of disconnect. Certainly, this has been true in my experience, both in my own marriage and in the marriages of the couples I've coached for more than thirty years.

Although many factors can initiate these transitions, you can tell you have reached a season of disconnect by the way you experience your partner. You may start to notice flaws in your spouse you never saw before. Or you may not even have major problems, but you won't feel that profound sense of being "in love" you once did. When you hit a season of marriage during which the original connection with your spouse fades, you can handle it in multiple ways.

One option is to accept the situation, scale down your expectations, and try to navigate an arrangement that works other than divorce. With this option, the couple is not necessarily committed to each other but is to the idea of their marriage. This commitment can be made out of moral, practical, or structural reasons and may result in varying degrees of happiness. However, it will not reignite the profundity of true love and the ultimate fulfillment of a phenomenal marriage.

A second option is to develop high-end problem-solving strategies, and negotiation and communication skills with high emphasis on one's partner's temperaments and compatibility. More often than not, obsessing over solving marriage problems stresses a relationship further. If you choose this option, in the best-case scenario, you solve some of your problems, communicate more effectively, and fight less frequently and in a more controlled and constructive manner. Instead of the passionate, awesome, powerful, deeply connected love you once experienced, you may succeed in negotiating a tolerable existence—but you won't feel as connected and complete as you once did.

A third option is to get a divorce, and begin a search for someone new. In truth, it takes far less time, effort, and money to learn to love the person you married than to divorce them and find somebody else. Statistically, your chances of divorcing the second time are higher than the first. This is because love has very little to do with picking the right person. *Your challenge is not to find the right person to love; it's to love the person you find.*

Your last option, and one that I suggest for most marriages, is the All-for-Nothing Marriage. With this option, you can reconnect with your spouse and rekindle love in your marriage. When you do, you'll fall in love all over again. In the second part of this book, I will describe just how to get there!

The hidden secret behind the season of disconnect in marriage is that ***nothing really changes in this space except love. Love is what changes your experience of everything.*** Your spouse and your compatibility do not change. It is the quality of the love in your marriage that changes how you experience those things. If you are lacking connection with your spouse, your experiences of each other will be negatively impacted. If you reconnect, you will regain the magic of your courtship.

The reason the All-for-Nothing Marriage works is that it focuses on reconnection and building love back into your relationship. The seasons of your marriage aren't triggered by the difficulties of life but by the manner in which you respond to them as a couple. If you address the root of your marriage and consummate a connection with your spouse, you will experience euphoric love and your problems will fade away. *Love conquers all. It is the root of transformation.*

I highly recommend Gary D. Chapman's *The Four Seasons of Marriage.* It is an excellent book that discusses the stages and changes in marriages. Any marriage guide would find this book very helpful.

NOTES & PERSONAL JOURNAL PAGE

_____

_____

_____

_____

_____

_____

_____

_____

_____

_____

_____

_____

Lesson 8: The Compatibility Myth

IT IS SAID that *the minimum requirements for a successful marriage are spiritual compatibility, character compatibility, communicational compatibility, and mutual attraction*. The idea is that the more similar your background, the more likely your compatibility, and the more likely your marriage will work. Families operate on different wavelengths, expectations, and temperaments. In this understanding of compatibility, marrying someone from a completely different family temperament endangers or complicates the hope of success.

Though no one should settle for a relationship that comes up short in any (or all) of these four areas, I fear that *succeeding in marriage has very little to do with compatibility*. Love is what people crave. Unconditional love is the root of all transformation in relationships. It is common that most couple's efforts for love are actually efforts for greater compatibility. But another marriage fear I hold is that *demanding compatibility puts unhealthy conditions on love*. In fact, improving compatibility to find love is like driving in the city of Ouagadougou in Burkina Faso, looking for the Eiffel Tower. You won't find it. You're in the wrong place.

If you build your marriage on compatibility, then when compatibility diminished in a season of life, you would have permission to end or escape the marriage, particularly if compatibility was established through matters of character or competency, as in: "We are compatible because we feel the same way about things and we contribute to each other in complementary ways."

But are you then required to maintain the same feelings about the same things and perform in the same ways through your whole life? And should you change at all, does the resulting change in compatibility threaten your unity?

Destroying the compatibility myth allows you to confidently make vows to one another that express "for better or worse, until death do us part." You are not threatened by matters of compatibility as your connection is not found there. The truth of the matter is, many people who searched and chose the "right person" from similar backgrounds to build a happy marriage are now happily divorced. If you're asking whether you're with the right person, you might be asking the wrong question.

To this point, I channel many marriage experts and unconventional marriage fitness coaches like Mort Fertel: Your challenge is to build a core connection with the person you find—not to find the right person to love. The love in your marriage filters how you experience your partner. When you're in love, your partner is compassionate. When you're not, your partner is harsh. But what's causing the change is the state of your connection—your love. Love is the solution to all relationship problems, the path to ultimate fulfillment in your marriage and in your life. Going forward, through these sessions and into your marriage, we will not demand compatibility in order to determine suitability. We will continually return to matters of the soul.

So, don't worry if you and your spouse aren't fully compatible. *You don't have to be compatible to be happily married; you have to be soulmates.* That's the *art* of love. Being soulmates is about forging a much more profound connection than interests or temperaments. It's about creating greater "stickiness" to the "glue" that Mother Nature provided.

Mort Fertel is the creator of the Marriage Fitness Tele-Boot Camp and author of *Marriage Fitness: Four Steps to Building and Maintaining Phenomenal Love.* Mort is a household name on social media these days with his alternative approach to counselling. Although unconventional, his Marriage Fitness Program is worth the time and investment.

NOTES & PERSONAL JOURNAL PAGE

Lesson 9: Why Aren't You More Like Me?

DIFFERENCES BETWEEN PEOPLE abound in marriage. These differences can first attract, then irritate, then frustrate, then illuminate, and finally unite us. Differences may manifest in two broad categories. Some, *such as age, race, looks, cultural background, etc., cannot be changed over time.* But there are *some differences that can change to reflect the constant upgrades created by your beliefs, experience, thoughts, education and learning, the significant events and trauma in your life, etc.* In marriage, you must adjust to both similarities and differences at the same time. It is often said that we marry for similarities but stay together for differences.

Many problems occur in the marital relationship because of a lack of tolerance for differences of attitude or opinion. *Neuroscience research, across the spectrum from animals to humans, supports the indication that our brain is binary. That it operates in black and white. This characteristic results in our tendency to minimize our commonalities while obsessing over our differences.* Additionally, we are often lazy in our relationships. This isn't a reflection of a lack of personal discipline. *It's biology.* Our brains are designed to survive and conserve energy. We are designed to find shortcuts, and subconsciously, we believe that if we can make our partners similar to us, they will be easier to manage.

But your partner is not you. He or she is a whole person, an "*other*," apart from you, created in God's image, not yours. Your partner has a right to be totally *other*, to be treated and respected as *other*. *The oneness in marriage is not ontological similarity or sameness, but functional oneness and understanding.* Any attempt to mould someone else to match our image of them is arrogance on our part and an insult to the integrity of their humanity.

When faced with the differences in your relationship, accept that at times you may try to accommodate, tolerate, overlook, or deny differences to avoid conflict. Then, at other times, you may challenge and try to eliminate the differences by demanding, demeaning, complaining, pressuring, or manipulating your spouse. But as you stay with it, you may eventually begin to appreciate the differences, to discover that they are necessary and indispensable. Suddenly, you may begin to welcome and celebrate your differences.

To assist you in fully discovering your uniqueness and differences, ask your guide, minister, or counsellor to administer the Personal Style Indicator (PSI). This tool provides a roadmap for knowing yourself better and understanding others. You can eliminate frustration by discovering now how God uniquely created you and how you can learn to be compatible with your spouse. The PSI helps you better understand your personality. It is the most accurate and insightful tool available to measure personality characteristics. It is also important to expand your understanding by reading about who you are. A book designed to help you understand personality, gender, and learning-style differences is *Why Aren't You More Like Me,* by Ken Keis with Everett Robinson.

NOTES & PERSONAL JOURNAL PAGE

Lesson 10: Marriage as a Vocation

MARRIAGE IS VOCATION. Typically, we think of vocation as a career. It is more than that. Vocation is a call over our lives that we must pursue to discover wholeness. Marriage is, therefore, a calling—not a requirement. All vocations are gifts to be received—not goals to be achieved. A true vocation does not divorce the nature of the human self from their service.

There are many people who believe that it is God's plan for everyone to get married. That's not the case. In fact, the Bible acknowledges that some people will choose not to marry (Jesus, Matthew 19:12). Jesus defends those who have renounced marriage because of the kingdom of heaven. This means that God gives capacity to those who remain single for a lifetime to enjoy that state. Through him, singleness can be a gift. This does not mean that every single person should choose to remain single forever but maybe just for a season. The most important thing for every single person is to submit his or her singleness to God and to use this singleness for as long as it lasts to serve God's purposes on Earth.

Gary Thomas challenges us when he asks with the title of his book: Sacred Marriage: What if God Designed Marriage to Make us Holy More than to Make Us Happy? Great question! What if God designed marriage to make us holy more than to make us happy? Perhaps, when a person chooses marriage, they also choose a tool that God can use to form and shape them in the image of God, to encourage and refresh the church, the bride of Christ.

Marriage provides a hospice in which we can explore ourselves with authenticity and vulnerability. However, marriage is not the answer for everyone. It is not for wimps. Marriage can add profoundly to your life, with meaningful dimension. But marriage will not satisfy your deepest human needs. It will not cure you of your inner loneliness. It will not heal your brokenness or ensure your happiness. Marriage has no guarantees, and if you approach it rooted in certain expectation, you may lose out.

Sadly, the most miserable people in the world are often not those who are single and wish to be married, but rather, married people who feel that their marriage was a tragic mistake. Fortunately, marriages that feel like tragic mistakes can often be redeemed, but it can require a staggering amount of work.

So, marriage is a vocation that is rooted in the deep gladness of knowing that we are here on earth as gifts that God created. In marriage we offer ourselves, body, mind, soul/heart, and spirit to another joyfully, not out of obligation. And as we do, we may find our most significant calling fulfilled.

NOTES & PERSONAL JOURNAL PAGE

_____

_____

_____

_____

_____

_____

_____

_____

_____

_____

_____

_____

Lesson 11: Why Your Marriage Will Kill You Before Death Do You Part.

IT WOULD HAVE benefited me greatly to know beforehand that getting married would kill me. Not in the physical sense, but in the sense that marriage requires you to die to the version of self that you are most familiar with. It demands becoming, freeing up, disentangling from anything that holds you back from giving authentically—without expectation or malice.

Luckily, marriage is by far the most fertile ground for personal formation. It is the ultimate relief to what is preventing you from becoming the purest form of yourself.

The version of who you are before marriage is untested. In my opinion, *marriage is the ultimate enema to relieve existential constipation. As such, it will demolish and dismantle all of the delusions you carry of yourself, unleashing the power of rebirth, as you morph to the more complete version of yourself—your irreducible minimum.* Sooner or later, your marriage will kill in you all manner of pride, unbridled selfishness and self-centredness, arrogance, entitlement, and untamed self-gratification.

And having gone through the refiner's fire, you'll prove a better, stronger person. You will shift your priorities, stop making everything about you, refuse to show up as a victim of life's circumstances, and learn to embrace agape love. In doing all of this you will have gained personal mastery, and mental control over self-centred impulses. You will see the reemergence of your own life—redemptive life. I assure you that marriage was the most effective tool to sculpt me to yet become a more complete version of me.

Recognize that dying to yourself requires not discounting yourself but embracing yourself more fully and abandoning all comparison to others.

Attempting to achieve an archetypal marriage based on hype and others' approval is violence against self. It will rob you of essential motivation and take your eye off the organic matter needed to transform your world for good.

Because the reality is that the Joneses aren't happy either, regardless of what they show on the surface. *And even if they are, **if you try to achieve your happiness the same way they do, you will not find it. That isn't your path. There is no ideal marriage anywhere on earth. Period.***

So, don't believe the hype and don't fake it. Don't listen to your "the Joneses." The grass is not greener on the other side. Most importantly, don't change who you are. Become *more* of who you are. For who you are will add distinct value to your marriage and the world.

Ultimately, your best marriage is not someone else's; it's yours. When you embrace your true lives, you will *become*, and your ideal versions will contribute your fullest to life everywhere.

But marriage is hard work. It is not for wimps! In truth, most times, I suck at being married. And like everyone else, my marriage has kicked the crap out of me.

But it turns out that all I needed was to adjust my mindset to one where I was never going to give up. Toward unfeigned love. I had to stick to marriage and suck at it long enough until I got better at it. Instead of thinking I wasn't good enough to get better, I gave myself space to become. And I am still becoming! With each season of marriage, I inch ever closer to living my dream life, accomplishing my ambitions, and earning the liberation—the lifestyle—I've always wanted.

So, when things get hard, simply put your head down and do the work. Die to all things that prevent you from connecting truly and soulfully to your partner. Embrace agape love and free yourself from expectation. It's 100 percent to none! It's an All-*for*-Nothing Marriage. If you want a marriage and a life that are better than anyone else's, you've gotta want them more and work on them harder than anyone else. The difference between who you are and who you want to be is your willingness to keep working at and/or for it. Your victory comes in the dying and the becoming.

NOTES & PERSONAL JOURNAL PAGE

_____

_____

_____

_____

_____

_____

_____

_____

_____

_____

_____

_____

_____

Lesson 12: Six Common Marriage Problems and How to Avoid Making Them Worse

THESE ARE SIX key concepts that I continually run into that push marriages off the smooth road and into a ditch—divorce on one side, a loveless and hopeless marriage on the other. I consider these my red flags to a disconnected relationship. Frequently, people aren't properly prepared for marriage, and consequently, they don't pay attention to each other's stories and/or are not present for one another daily. Further, they don't do conflict well because they don't effectively validate themselves or one another and are obsessed with problem-solving. These may also be seen as six potholes that can lead your marriage to ruin.

FEAR OF CONFLICT

All relationships have conflict, and the healthiest people know how to approach it rather than avoid it. Conflict is not bad. Poorly managed conflict is terrible, but worst of all is conflict not had. Conflict happens in every great love story, in every relationship, and it is going to happen to you in your relationship, too. Doing conflict well may be the difference between living happily ever after and calling it quits.

Because most people learn how to do conflict (or not) by what they observed growing up, we don't believe we can navigate it in a successful way. This lack of trust, in both our own and our partner's reactions, prevents us from engaging in open, constructive, ideological conflict. The success to navigating conflict is to trust, be vulnerable, and validate and honour your partner without prejudice.

INVALIDATION

In healthy relationships, couples self-validate and validate one another. Self-validation occurs when you are able to quietly reassure yourself that what you feel inside is real, is important, and makes sense. Likewise, giving validation to another means acknowledging that what they feel, think, believe, and experience is real, logical, understandable. Validation does NOT mean that you AGREE or APPROVE of behaviour; in fact, validation is non-judgmental. In healthy relationships, couples become effective at validating themselves and each other, because when they do, the quality of the relationship gets better. Validation quiets defensive/fearful emotions so that we can let go of the pain and exhaustion that constant self-justification and self-doubt require, problem-solve, and deal with conflict/crisis effectively. When we fail to validate/self-validate, or even worse, when we invalidate one another, it can break the connections we build as couples and lead to distrust, poor or unhealthy forms of communication, and resentment.

INATTENTION TO THE COLLECTIVE STORYLINE

Marriage is the coming together of two stories, the joining of two settings. The more you know about the setting of your partner's story, the better your collective story will be. Failure to appreciate the critical scenes that feed and shape each other's stories may prove fatal, because when you don't understand your spouse's story, you cannot know them. Without knowing who your partner is, you may be inclined to attempt to fix or alter them in a way that is relevant or makes sense to your story but not to theirs. In this space, you can effectively "tell" your partner who to be and thus murder them from their personhood. This scenario can lead any marriage to ruin.

POOR PREPARATION

Quite often, people come into marriage with lousy goals and unhealthy expectations. A healthy goal is one where the end result can be achieved by you alone. A lousy goal is one that requires someone else to be achieved. Many couples enter marriage seeking to make their partner happy. Truth be told, this is a lousy goal as it is not possible to make your partner happy without their permission. To contrast this, a good goal would be to support your partner in pursuing their own happiness. This is something achievable by oneself.

In addition to poor goal-setting, many couples enter marriage with pre-designed expectations of what their partners will become to them. By doing this, we design a space to interpret the actions and words of our partner through that lens. Instead of allowing our partners to be who they are, we create an idealized version of who we want them to be. By having these expectations, we cause our real partner to compete with our idealization of them. Lousy goal-setting and unhealthy expectations compromise the foundation on which we build our relationships and lead marriages toward failure.

ABSENCE OF SOUL

Most marriages suffer because the people in them have checked out. When asked, most people say they checked out long before settling for divorce. To build an amazing marriage you are summoned to be present with all your body, mind, heart/soul, and spirit. Sadly, most couples do not live in the now. They live somewhere in nightmares, imagination, and regret from their past, depleting their marriage of the life-giving energy of their presence. Committing to be present is crucial for the success of marriage. Failure to show up for your partner—and by extension, yourself—will result in your drifting apart and eventually separating. You can measure a couple's success by the level of generosity and care they provide to each other.

ADDICTION TO PROBLEM-SOLVING

Most relationships are plagued with problems. When problems arise in a marriage, our first impulse is to set out to solve them problem-solving is a natural tendency of our social behaviour. Some people are obsessive problem-solvers. They devotedly create and solve problems, because without problems in need of solving, they lose their purpose. Someone said that upward of 80 percent of the problems in most marriages will never, ever be solvable. They may be perpetual, forever grounded in the fundamental differences that any two people face. Sometimes, talking about the problems in a marriage makes them worse. As is often said, you'll never talk yourself out of a problem that you behaved yourself into. Redemptive choices resolve marital problems;

talking doesn't. In hostile environments, compulsive problem-solving can push your marriage off the smooth road and into a ditch. The question is not how to solve your problems. The key to a successful marriage is primary love, and that's what this book is all about.

NOTES & PERSONAL JOURNAL PAGE

_____

_____

_____

_____

_____

_____

_____

_____

_____

_____

_____

_____

PART 2:

THE ALL-FOR-NOTHING
MARRIAGE — FOUR-STEP PLAN

Summary

WE'VE ARRIVED AT the million-dollar question: How do you create that bond of unity that results in primary love and ultimate fulfillment in life? The answer is Part Two of this book, the All-*for*-Nothing Marriage Four-Step Plan.

This section will give you practical ideas for rekindling that core connection that results in phenomenal love and ultimate fulfillment in life. I have brought the lessons with which the Lord has blessed me along my journey. I am turning them over to you.

Part Two of this book will challenge you to develop positive attitudes and actions that will greatly enhance the climate of your marriage in ways that will affect both you and your spouse.

It will do so in four steps that focus on:

1. Understanding love and how to make it the centre of your relationship.

2. Learning how to effectively connect with your partner.

3. Shifting your perspective to achieve success in your marriage.

4. Accepting that your best is all you need to have a meaningful life together.

By mastering and applying these four disciplines, you can ensure that your own marriage will thrive. You'll learn to identify which of these components is a weak spot—or a potential weak spot—in your relationship, and to focus your attention where you most need it. In the chapters ahead, we'll fill you in on all the secrets to maintaining (or regaining) a happy marriage, and hold your hand as you apply the disciplines to your own relationship.

Put Love First
(STEP ONE)

STEP ONE OF *The* All-*for*-Nothing *Marriage Method* is to put love first. This step is a prerequisite for all of the other steps. Your marriage has to be the highest priority in your life in order for you to have the time and energy for steps two, three, and four.

NOTES & PERSONAL JOURNAL PAGE

_____

_____

_____

_____

_____

_____

_____

_____

_____

_____

_____

_____

Lesson 1: Put Love First

LOVE IS THE dominant force in the universe; it determines the experience of your life. Therefore, love should come first. If you want to build a meaningful marriage, with all your mind, with all your soul, with all your might, *put love first*. If you don't *put love first*, you will not be fulfilled. If you p*ut love first,* you take the biggest leap to transforming your marriage and your life.

Love is made up of nine ingredients: patience, kindness, generosity, humility, courtesy, unselfishness, good temper, guilelessness, and joyful sincerity. Love is not a permanent state of enthusiasm.

Paul said, "If I have all faith, so that I can remove mountains, and have not love, I am nothing." So, although we have been accustomed to being told that the greatest thing in the religious world is faith, in reality, faith, eloquence, prophecy, and any other thing pales in comparison with love.

Love alone can conquer the human heart. It is the strongest power. It never fails, never gives up, and never runs out. True love demands we be and become more fully ourselves. It is love that shapes whatever is true, whatever is noble, whatever is right, whatever is pure, whatever is admirable, excellent, or praiseworthy. Love alone bears all things, believes all things, hopes all things, endures all things. Love covers over a multitude of sins (Paul, 1 Corinthians 13).

We know very little about the conditions of the life to come. But what is certain is that love is going to stand forever. Where love is, God is. If you dwell in love, you dwell in God. Everyone that loves is born of God. This is the foundation of the gospel, the good news to the world. Through the course of this life, we all end up giving ourselves to many things, but love is the one thing we must give ourselves to. When we do, we hold things in their proportion. Love is supreme.

I recommend Henry Drummond's *The Greatest Thing in the World*, first published in 1890. I was fortunate to get my hand on the 1980 edition, and it did me lots of good. These are Drummond's commentaries on Paul's Hymn of Love (1 Corinthians 13).

NOTES & PERSONAL JOURNAL PAGE

_____

_____

_____

_____

_____

_____

_____

_____

_____

_____

_____

_____

_____

Lesson 2: Prioritize Your Marriage

PEOPLE TAKE FOR granted that love comes easily, mostly because that's what Hollywood portrays. But the movies aren't reality. Love requires time, effort, and attention to maintain in the long term. *Love comes easily during courtship, but that is because, at first, Mother Nature is on your side. Unfortunately, she doesn't stick around to help forever.* After a couple of years, those batteries die and she leaves it up to you to keep your marriage charged. When things reach this point, you need to *make* that love connection yourself, and it's going to take effort. It doesn't come freely as a gift anymore.

Once the honeymoon phase wanes, you may find your focus is no longer solely on your partner, and that your priorities have drifted. And with this drifting, you may lose that sense of connection. But reinvigorating your connection in this case isn't as hard as you may think. At this stage, all you really need to do is shift back your priority.

John Mordecai Gottman is an American psychological researcher and clinician who did extensive work over four decades on divorce prediction and marital stability. He is also an award-winning speaker and author, and a professor emeritus in psychology. In his book, *The Seven Principles for Making Marriage Work*, he explains that we tend to think of infidelity in sexual terms. However, he argues that an extramarital physical affair is only one type of disloyalty that threatens a relationship. He says we need to think of betrayal as, fundamentally, any act or life choice that doesn't prioritize the commitment and put the partner "before all others." The key, he suggested, is in learning how to better attune to each other and make friendship a top priority.

Certainly, your priority is something you need to constantly be straight about, because it is the crucial factor to transform your marriage. How you select what you prioritize is one of the best tools you have to either build or destroy connections. For, when you *prioritize your partner,* it will manifest feelings of love for them naturally. And if you *feel prioritized* as a partner, you automatically feel loved. Thus, prioritizing your partner is an action you can choose that will result in the regeneration of that feeling of love and commitment.

You don't need to turn your whole life upside down to embrace this concept. Simply make your marriage more important than anything else: church, business, or other pursuits. This requires paying devoted, unadulterated attention. Sometimes, professional demands and personal ambitions result in people working more and spending less time with family. In pursuit of wealth, pleasure, or fame, one or both partners become immersed in their jobs and end up neglecting each other. When this happens, couples become unavailable to each other. What began as a passionate love story becomes sidelined. This creates silent frustration within the marriage, which morphs to silent protest.

But when you change your priority, you transform your life. Cleanse your life of anything that prevents you from focusing on your marriage. Mort Fertel makes this point better than anyone I've read on this, in his Marriage Fitness classes: Whatever you prioritize, you'll end up giving your soul to. Prioritize something other than your relationship and you'll be married to it instead. So, simply decide to order your life in such a way that your marriage is the highest priority in your life and immediately begin to behave in ways that reflect that priority. That's the only change you need to make for a meaningful marriage.

John Gottman identified four pillars of meaning to help you make your marriage a priority. He found that the more shared meaning couples can build, the deeper, richer, and more rewarding their relationship became. He highlighted four critical pillars of meaning that enrich relationships and family life: rituals, supporting each other's roles, shared goals, and a shared philosophy of life (values and symbols).

In particular, he lamented how we have sidelined critical rituals of connecting and traded them for social media. A ritual is a structured event or routine that you each enjoy and depend on and that both reflects and reinforces your sense of togetherness. Most of us are familiar with rituals from our childhood, like regular dinners together, date night, church services, family reunions, Christmas Eve, lighting Kwanzaa candles or the menorah, Thanksgiving, etc. Creating rituals in your marriage (and with your children) can be a powerful way to prioritize your marriage by building meaning together and maximizing connection. It is our priority in the next pages to help you prioritize your marriage. Keep reading.

I recommend John Gottman's *The Seven Principles for Making Marriage Work*. Any marriage guide would find this book very helpful. It is full of assessments and tools that can be used as enriching conversations

I also recommend Mort Fertel, creator of the Marriage Fitness Tele-Boot Camp and author of *Marriage Fitness: Four Steps to Building and Maintaining Phenomenal Love*.

NOTES & PERSONAL JOURNAL PAGE

_____

_____

_____

_____

_____

_____

_____

_____

_____

_____

_____

_____

_____

_____

_____

Lesson 3: Understand the Inner-Workings of primary love

EARLIER, WE DESCRIBED primary love as the giving of oneself away freely, irrespective of the worthiness of the recipient. This entire session offers insights into the inner workings of primary love

Love and giving go hand in hand. Giving creates love and a deep connection. The best example is the love and deep connection that parents feel for their children. Parenting is an exercise in perpetual unconditional giving. And there is almost no greater love than the love a parent feels for their child. Giving builds a connection between you and your spouse and creates the experience of love. And ironically, when you give, you get everything you need.

Genuine love, like the love a parent has for their child, is surrendered as a gift to God first, and the receiver second. When love is given this way, it frees the giver from any sense of expectation of return, as the gift is primarily a love offering to God Himself. This manner of giving love is what empowers the giver to do so with full freedom and joy. When our love is yielded to God, it is He who takes it and multiplies it. So, our love becomes not our own but rather His, manifested. This also reduces dependency on the receiver's love. Instead, we are fully sustained by the love of God, which is enough.

For the most part, a gift with expectation is way too dangerous to be received. We can use an analogy to understand further. Inuit people are said to hunt wolves by putting a bloody knife in the snow. The wolves come and lick the bloody knife, and as they begin to lick, they cut their tongues and then start tasting their own blood. They become so bloodthirsty that they eventually lick the knife to their death. A gift with expectation is like a bloody knife to a wolf. This kind of gift can become a cyclical event and it is too expensive to receive. We keep receiving these gifts and they keep producing undesirable results until we *sober up a*nd drop them. Some gifts are just too costly. Giving with expectation is not at the heart of primary love.

NOTES & PERSONAL JOURNAL PAGE

_____

_____

_____

_____

_____

_____

_____

_____

_____

_____

_____

_____

_____

_____

Lesson 4: 5 Love Gifts That Do More Damage Than Good

PRIMARY LOVE IS the *giving of oneself away freely, irrespective of the worthiness of the recipient.* This lesson offers further insights into the inner workings of primary love. To determine whether something is a good or a bad gift, you must evaluate the manner or spirit in which it's given, the hook behind it (if any), and whether it empowers or diminishes the giver and receiver. You must examine if the gift is given:

joyfully, not begrudgingly. If the gift is not given joyfully, do not receive it. Each one must give as he has decided in his heart, not reluctantly or under compulsion, for God loves a cheerful giver (Paul, 2 Corinthians 9:7). The spirit in which a gift is given is more important than the gift itself. Remember, when it is a true gift, it is surrendered unto God first (the source of all blessing), then given to its ultimate recipient. If you give without surrender, you spoil the gift, you enslave the world.

without expectation. A giver should not expect anything from the receiver. Instead, the giver expects showers of blessings and a bountiful return from God, who is the source of all life and goodness, through our knowledge of Him. Whoever is generous to the poor lends to the Lord, and He will repay him for his deed (Solomon, Proverbs 19:17). He is a rewarder of faithfulness, the rewarder of those who diligently seek Him (Paul, Hebrew 11:6). When you give a gift, you deal directly with God, not the recipient of your gift.

with the intent to empower. A gift should be given with no intention to disempower another. Gifts, used incorrectly, can incite a sense of servitude or prostitution in the receiver. Gifts of this kind violate the giver's integrity while undermining the receiver's worth. Gifts given of this form shrink motivation. They do not add value but diminish it.

out of what you have. Make sure that whatever you intend to give is already in you. When you give out of what is truly inside you to give, you bless the world. You give out of rest, not out of anxiety. Whenever you try to give what you do not possess, it results in burnout. When you try to give out of what does not naturally grow within you, you deplete yourself and harm everyone around you. Every gift that is forced results in harm. When you reach the limit of your own capacity to love and give, you ought to trust divine providence—that someone else will be available to the person in need.

from a healthy place. A true gift can heal the world but to have redemptive power, the gift can only come from a place of health. When a giver fails to grieve or address previous losses, the gifts they present are contaminated with wounds from the past. Although the intent of a gift can be to heal, you will have no grace to do so. Gifts of this nature generate the opposite of their intention. They deplete the other, or produce violence, grief, and all manner of destruction.

NOTES & PERSONAL JOURNAL PAGE

Lesson 5: You Might Lose Out!

WE ARE STILL talking about primary love, the *giving of oneself away freely, irrespective of the worthiness of the recipient.* This lesson adds to the insights of the inner workings of primary love. **The back end of adopting primary love and a 100-to-none mentality is that there are no guarantees.** In the end, you might lose out! Saint Paul said that, if anyone unequally yoked themselves to someone of another faith or of no faith at all, the believer should not initiate any divorce proceeding toward the unbeliever. The believer is to honour, love, and respect their spouse regardless of faith matters. However, if the unbelieving partner desires to separate, the person of faith should make peace with the person of non-faith and proceed with divorce (St. Paul, 1 Corinthians 7:10-16).

What Paul is really describing here is a 100-to-none mentality. Regardless of your partner's visible differences and shortcomings, you are to love unconditionally and be devoted to them wholeheartedly. Not only that, but this devotion and love do not bind your partner to you. If they want to leave, they are free to go. *Sometimes, you may lose! Most people are so afraid of losses. As a result, they try to control everything. But love given with conditions and expectations, as we already know, is not love at all.*

It is important to be clear that, in this concept, the outcome of a marriage is irrelevant. You do not adopt a 100-to-None mentality to ensure that your marriage is wonderful. You do it because it is your vocation—your calling to do it. It is your Nazarite vow; you are doing this unto God, not unto your partner (this would be equally true if you had chosen singleness as your vow). You are doing this as an example of Christ and His Church. **There is something bigger going on than just your personal experience. Does that guarantee your marriage? No. But God doesn't call us to *be* in order to receive guarantees.**

However, by taking the path unto God, you have the absolute best shot at success in marriage. This is your best opportunity for a great outcome. The probability of success with 100-to-none is going to be way up. The other strategy is to give yourself to your partner 50/50. But this strategy will likely lead to one ditch or the other. How are you to give what is not yours? You can't give your humanness, your sexuality, your Christianity away. You can't let someone who is in a marriage destroy your personhood, because these are in the domain of God.

Additionally, even though you can give 100-to-none, there is no guarantee that your partner will always treat you well. Some people are toxic. They are so wounded that they destroy other people. No relationship has a right to destroy those parts of you that you bring to it. Your selfhood or humanness, your vows, your faith are sacred. Those are the foundation you bring to the marriage. They are the realm of the divine. *Your integrity must prevail. You have no right to let your partner destroy you. So, you are called to love and give without expectation in your marriage. The integrity of the self must be preserved.* Marriage does not come with guarantees.

NOTES & PERSONAL JOURNAL PAGE

_____

_____

_____

_____

_____

_____

_____

_____

_____

_____

_____

_____

_____

Lesson 6: Count to One

MARRIAGE FACILITATES TWO integral people coming together to create a meaningful social synergy.

Two become one in love—the creation of a whole that is greater than the sum of its parts. Synergy is accomplished by moving the centre of your life from "me" to "we," by intentionally decreasing "me" and increasing "we."

Someone once pointed out to me that to change the word "me" to "we," you flip the "m" upside down. This is the art of loving—*making a space in your life for another person.* Sometimes, that means your life gets turned upside down.

Unity is at the heart of marriage. When you create high-level togetherness, you build lasting love. But a house divided against itself cannot stand. When you live mostly outside the context of your marriage, you do so at the expense of your unity. Your life becomes so full there is simply no room for another person. Marriage requires a team effort.

The unity of the marriage mirrors that of God Himself. The Father, Son, and Holy Spirit are considered one in essence, but are all still functionally distinct. The same unity is dramatized in marriage. Two distinctive people join and become essentially one, yet functionally, two individual selves. A central moral imperative of marriage is this: *Marriage must not dissolve each of the persons who create it.* Marriage must never interfere with preserving self. Each person must retain his/her individual identity while drawing close together in meaningful relationship as one, under God.

In marriage, as one, you create love in your joys, burdens, flaws, differences, and tragedies together. You trade your problems for love. You do not seek blame or assign faults. You focus on solving all problems as one, united. When you do, you use your problems to join yourselves together, not divide apart. Together, you count as one! **The essential nature of marriage** is unity—a oneness and *existential togetherness* that exist in God. This oneness turns mediocre marriages into meaningful ones.

In a marriage, problems are neutral. It is how you handle your problems as a couple that can either destroy or create love. If you are on the same team, you can live with anything. If you're not, the slightest problem will drive you apart. When you operate as one, you magically transform the problem from one that divides you into one that unites you. To create love, you don't have to solve your problems, you only have to resolve your togetherness. Love conquers all.

NOTES & PERSONAL JOURNAL PAGE

_____

_____

_____

_____

_____

_____

_____

_____

_____

_____

_____

_____

_____

Tune in to the Frequency of Your Spouse
(STEP TWO)

STEP ONE OF The All-*for*-Nothing Marriage Method is to put love first. The second step is to Tune in to the Frequency of Your Spouse. Couples who *tune* to each other build critical connection and mutual trust. Those who don't are likely to lose their way.

NOTES & PERSONAL JOURNAL PAGE

Lesson 1: Give Soulful Presence

A CRUCIAL PLAN for connecting your cores and building amazing love is to give to your spouse, but specifically, to give presence. Presence is the rarest and purest form of generosity. It requires bestowing special attention on someone and making their presence count. The most important thing about a present is that it embodies the presence of the one who gave it to you. When you get a gift from someone you love, you love it not only because of what it is but because of who gave it to you.

Phenomenal marriages require time, non anxious presence and unfeigned attention. Studies show that making enough time for a marriage is key to making your relationship a happy and prosperous one. Giving presence is not just about making sure to spend time together; it's about decreasing the anxiety level, paying unadulterated attention to your partner and under-standing what they're going through.

Often, our contributions to the world, especially through the work we do and roles we play, are deprived of the life-giving energies of true presence. This means that we are physically present but mentally absent. A lack of presence can also show up when we make ourselves available out of duty or obligation, which robs our partner of the experience of our true authentic selves.

When our true selves are absent in these spaces, we are fraudulent. We are living a divided life. When this occurs, we have left our soul behind. Just as you need to eat regularly to give your body nourishment, you need to give to your soulmate regularly to give your marriage its fuel. Be here and now! In the words of Ralph Waldo Emerson, "The only gift is a portion of thyself." In marriage, the most important love gift is your presence.

NOTES & PERSONAL JOURNAL PAGE

_____

_____

_____

_____

_____

_____

_____

_____

_____

_____

_____

_____

_____

_____

Lesson 2: Become Soulmates Not Rolemates

CONNECTING IS THE key to creating love, but in order to connect with your spouse, you need to know where in your marriage to create that connection.

What part of you, when connected with the corresponding part of your spouse, is transformative? In other words, where does love happen? To get there, you need to find the soul of your mate!

Being soulmates has very little to do with performance and demanding character change. Judgment and feelings of inadequacy or superiority are often the result of character comparisons. But when the focus of your marriage is a core connection, there's nothing to measure. Every soul is incomparable. For soulmates, character flaws are mitigated by the fact that the marriage is not based on its participants' characters. Character compatibility is certainly not bad. However, *compatibility and love are as far apart as east and west. As William Shakespeare said, "soulful love bears it out even to the edge of doom." Soulmates are not perfect for each other. Soulmates love each other with all their imperfections. Soulmates love each other no matter what.*

When you and your spouse connect at your cores, you experience life very differently than you would if your marriage was based on character compatibility. Soulmates are natural with each other. They give out of what is organic to them—out of the "seed" of true self that is planted in the world at their birth. They're not trying to impress each other. In fact, the deeper a couple's core connection, the freer they are to be themselves and the less impressive they may appear to each other. Whenever you try to give what you do not possess, it will result in burnout. You violating your own nature in the name of nobility doesn't add value to anyone. When you give out of what is organic to you, your giving creates abundance, renewing itself—and you— even as you give it away. Success in love takes more than working harder on character; it takes wisdom. You have to know where to direct your efforts. Transformative love comes from your core, not from character improvement. Direct your efforts there.

Simply put, the key to making love is to shift focus from demanding character change to connecting at your cores. In other words, stop fooling with your problems and start becoming soulmates. That's your solution.

I recommend Parker J. Palmer's *Let Your Life Speak: Listening for the Voice of Vocation*. It is an excellent book that discusses vocation, and in particular, giving out of true self. It is one of my favourite books in the world. I read it at least once per year!

And then, again, there's Mort Fertel of the Marriage Fitness Tele-Boot Camp and author of *Marriage Fitness: Four Steps to Building and Maintaining Phenomenal Love* speaks passionately about the universal principles of love, unity, intimacy, and connection. I find his teachings very practical and inspiring.

NOTES & PERSONAL JOURNAL PAGE

Lesson 3: Sometimes the Soul Escapes the Body

IT IS SAID that Livingston, who was a missionary in Africa, was once on a journey with his crew. As they hurried along to get to their destination, one of the men on the journey, an elderly fellow, suddenly dropped the luggage he was carrying under a tree, found a log, and sat on it. He had an existential problem. When Livingston and the crew asked him what had caused this erratic behaviour, the man gazed at them and said in a somber voice, "You put too much pressure on me. I walked so fast and have come so far only to realize I have left my soul behind. I will not move a single inch further till my soul comes back to my body."

We certainly have something to learn from this wise man! We, too, as a people—as a society—have come so far only to discover that we have left our soul behind.

When this happens, we turn to the divided life—a wounded life—to which the soul keeps calling us to heal the wound. When we ignore the soul and that deep call to wholeness, we find ourselves trying to numb our pain with an anesthetic of choice, be it substance abuse, overwork, consumerism, or mindless media noise. Such medicators are easy to come by in a society that is designed to keep us divided and unaware of our pain. The greatest existential struggle, the largest plight for any human being, is to give primacy to those things that matter most to us. This can be difficult when we are surrounded by propaganda that pushes the solutions for our brokenness outward.

We are born with a seed of selfhood that contains the spiritual DNA of our uniqueness: Our soul or true self is the objective, ontological reality of selfhood. This ontological reality alone keeps us from reducing ourselves, or each other, to mere biological mechanisms, psychological projections, sociological constructs, or raw material to be manufactured into whatever society needs. Our true self carries the encoded birthright knowledge of who and why we are here. We may abandon that knowledge as the years go by, but it never abandons us. We may lose touch with our souls and disappear into our roles, become masked and armoured at considerable cost to self, others, and the world at large. When we do, we feel fraudulent, even invisible, because we are not in the world as who we really are. Our inauthenticity and projections make real relationships impossible, leading to loneliness. The light that is within us cannot illuminate the world's darkness. The darkness that is within us cannot be illuminated by the world's light. We project our inner darkness on others, making "enemies" of them and making the world a more dangerous place.

Marriage can have the capacity to both build and pull apart the soul by either affirming personhood or distracting from one's purpose through the pursuit of expectation. Your duty in marriage is both to self and mate: To support your friend in pursuing their calling, and in doing so, finding yours. It is easy to focus on building an external life that supports the ideals and priorities of society. However, without maintaining cognizance of the importance of preserving self, couples can become resentful, having built separate paths that pull them away from their core and make them lose themselves.

To learn more about the undivided life and rejoining soul and role, I recommend Parker J. Palmer's book, *A Hidden Wholeness: The Journey Toward an Undivided Life.*

NOTES & PERSONAL JOURNAL PAGE

Lesson 4: The Sacrament of Touch

MOST PEOPLE ACKNOWLEDGE that touch provides significant psychological benefits, but few recognize that it is also a requirement for healthy physical development. Psychogenic dwarfism, or deprivation dwarfism, is a syndrome in which children develop an extremely short stature and voracious appetite, and have a marked delay in sexual maturation as a result of both emotional and physical deprivation. When a child is emotionally and physically starved, their "normal" hormone secretion patterns are disrupted, and their proper development is suspended. It has been found that, without touch, no medical intervention is sufficient to nurture the child back to health.

This phenomenon is also reported in animals. When deprived and under-stimulated, young mammals develop abnormally. Some fail to urinate or defecate and soon die of toxicity. Without proper touch, it seems, certain autonomic bodily functions cannot be established, and growth does not proceed normally. Touch is critical to our physical development.

Touch is also important for our overall psychology. When humans touch one another, our bodies release oxytocin. Oxytocin is a hormone linked to various behaviours. It plays a role in facilitating trust and attachment between individuals; it can reduce fear, has antidepressant-like effects, increases feelings of generosity and empathy, is correlated with romantic attachment, orgasm, social recognition, and maternal behaviour, and reduces inflammation to speed healing. In addition to oxytocin, when we are in love, our bodies produce dopamine, a hormone that creates feelings of pleasure. Your serotonin levels, on the other hand, reportedly drop when you're in love. And since serotonin helps you stay calm, its decrease results in feelings of nervousness and excitement. Your brain also releases phenylethylamine, or PEA—otherwise known as the "love molecule."

But the power of these chemicals lessens over time, which is another part of the reason attraction fades. There's a reason new relationships are so much fun. Indeed, in those early stages of romance, your body produces the same chemicals that addiction triggers: intense feelings of attraction, butterflies in your stomach, lightheadedness, and a loss of appetite. All are responses to chemicals your body releases when you're in love.

What all this boils down to is that the more you touch your partner, the closer your bond. So, don't skimp on the cuddling and hugging, or on the amazing sex! Fortunately, it's possible to influence your own biochemistry—and thus improve your relationship! There is power in touch! So, touch a little more.

NOTES & PERSONAL JOURNAL PAGE

Lesson 5: Develop Empathic Listening

IN MY EXPERIENCE, we are more frequently storytellers than we are story listeners. This is because the most primitive parts of us seek community through sharing stories. However, one of the most tragic laments of our time is that "no one really sees me, hears me, or understands me." This is because we get so caught up telling and don't set ourselves aside to listen. In marriage, one of the most important offerings we can ever make is to really listen to our partner's stories!

My fascination with stories got its start in my youth in Yoro, a village in western Africa. In this oral culture, with its stock of canonical life narratives, storytelling was at the heart of daily life. Also, as a minister, I have heard countless stories from the people I've served.

People have many stories that constitute their identities: who they are in the world, how they became who they are, and how they make meaning of their personal experiences. Stories are powerful forces for good and for ill!

As creative explanations, people's stories become their reality. Stories have the ability to break down walls, get us to care, and make us think differently. And in so doing, they have the power to ignite change. Good stories ground the world in truth. If you change the story you're telling yourself, you will experience something different.

Whatever story you are telling yourself is producing the feelings that govern your life right now. Life is full of challenges and sometimes even tragedies. We redeem these difficult things by finding a perspective on them that betters our lives through storytelling.

The way to avoid or reduce drama and stress in your life is to master your stories, to break from the ones that are based on fear and make you feel powerless. It is possible to re-perceive the world and your relationship to it, to extend your capacity to create, to be part of the generative process of life.

Empathic listening redeems people

Empathic listening is powerful. It is an act that symbolizes that you are present and tuned in. It creates empathy, reveals commitment, and affirms relationship. Listening also provides a safe space for the unveiling of your partner's soul and the drama within. Listening is the greatest act of validation. And validation is a pillar in the foundation of a healthy relationship.

Good communication depends on you carefully listening to another person and becoming more tolerant of each other's imperfections. Empathic listening involves listening attentively without interruption and then restating what was heard. The empathic listening process lets the storyteller know whether the spoken message was clearly understood by restating what they heard.

Listening exposes and tests what is in your heart. It can touch off or reveal previous personal wounds. If performed correctly, listening has the capacity to help heal these wounds. If done incorrectly, it can invalidate the storyteller and pull relationship apart. Sadly, because our stories make us vulnerable to being fixed, exploited, dismissed, or ignored, we have learned to tell them guardedly or not at all. It is when your thinking (the mind) and emotions (the heart) are most inflamed that listening is tested and becomes critical. There is a method to listening effectively in a hostile environment.

First, you must get out of your own echo-chambers. It is easy to defend a person's' constitutional rights when you agree with the person! But the test of listening is this: Can you honour someone with whom you don't agree?

Second, assume people mean well. We often judge ourselves by our best intentions but judge others by their actions. What if we listen generously? What if we began with their best intentions?

Third, avoid judgment. Even if you feel like you are being lied to, listen. Ignore emotions, suspend feeling. Be freed from the need to identify or agree. Don't move to assign blame or support. Non-judgmental story-listening is one of the most important and vital skills in anyone's life, for it holds the key to relationships, success, and influence.

Fourth, overcome your need to correct and educate. The habit of fixing, saving, advising, and setting each other straight has such a powerful grip on our lives. In truth, we often listen critically. We rush to "repair," to escape the pain, woundedness, or fear we see reflected from our own stories in theirs. The shadow behind the "fixes" we offer is, ironically, the desire to hold each other at bay. It is a strategy for abandoning each other while appearing to be concerned. We must learn to listen to each other's core and not fix.

Listening restores people's sobriety of mind and state. Great listening is evident when you help others prove their point. You validate, not educate. You are free from the need to be right. Great listening creates intimacy. Intimacy creates authentic community. Authentic community heals the world.

NOTES & PERSONAL JOURNAL PAGE

_____

_____

_____

_____

_____

_____

_____

_____

_____

_____

_____

_____

_____

Lesson 6: Learn to Speak Your Spouse's Language

STORYTELLING IS AT the heart of being human, because it serves some of our most basic needs: passing along traditions, confessing failings, healing wounds, engendering hope, and strengthening our sense of community. *But stories are also our maps of the world.* As creative explanations, stories shape our imagination, help us make sense of the world around us, and have the incredible ability to stimulate connections, empathy, and understanding, and drive change. Stories are powerful motivational forces that affect what we do because they affect what we see. Each story we tell ourselves creates powerful mental images: assumptions of other people, ourselves, institutions, God, and every aspect of the world.

But not all storytelling is healthy or helpful. When wounded, humans have the tendency to operate in worse-case scenarios, to see our differences and not our similarities, and to judge ourselves by our best intentions and others by their worst. When these dysfunctions are present in our stories, they become sick. The stories you tell yourself and your partner can empower you or crush your confidence. When we tell sick stories in our relationships, they produce high levels of distrust, and deplete compassion, generosity, and care. In fact, sick stories, on a high or wide enough platform, are powerful enough to make an entire nation sick, to create genocides and wars. People are as healthy as the stories they tell.

The cure to sick storytelling is redemptive storytelling. In marriages, redemptive storytelling manifests when you speak in your spouse's primary love language. Redemptive storytelling presumes that people mean their best. And that, even if their best isn't enough, they are giving all they can afford. This kind of storytelling is sacrificial. It is a gift you give, especially when someone does not deserve it. It's meant to be given to others and yourself. Redemptive storytelling is rooted in forgiveness and grace. It shapes events into narratives of hope. When you operate like this, you manifest the 100-to-none mindset and produce a meaningful marriage.

To me, every story is a prophetic imagination. You draw the meaning of your life from the stories you tell yourself. Whatever story you're telling yourself is producing the feelings that make up your living reality, thinking, and behaviour. This means you may not blame your partner for your feelings. Take responsibility over your stories and feelings and you will change your experience of life forever.

Lastly, it is important to understand that, *because our stories make us vulnerable to being fixed, exploited, dismissed, or ignored, we have learned to tell many of them guardedly or sometimes not at all. Withholding our stories is a barrier against building intimacy in relationships and can prevent us from achieving true connection with our partners.* So, tell your stories, but tell them redemptively! When couples make it a discipline to retell their stories redemptively, magical connection manifests at the soul level.

I recommend *The Five Love Languages,* by Gary Chapman. *The Five Love Languages* is an excellent book that discusses comprehensively the topic at hand. Chapman suggests that each person has a primary love language and that we must learn to speak the language of our partner if we want that person to feel loved.

These languages are:

1. Words of affirmation: spoken praise and appreciation.

2. Acts of service: Actions speak louder than words. "Doing" to help your spouse—ASK your spouse, "What is helping?"

3. Receiving gifts: Little things mean a lot. Birthdays, holidays, anniversaries, and "no occasion" days.

4. Quality time: Giving undivided attention—turn off the TV, look into your spouse's eyes, listen and interact.

5. Physical touch: Take the initiative to reach out and touch. Hand on shoulder while you walk, holding hands, touching leg while you drive together, kissing, embracing, sexual intercourse.

Understanding and speaking your spouse's love language may not be easy at first. You learn to speak a new love language by trying, trying, and again trying. This discipline of making this effort to speak in your spouse's primary love language is the byproduct of unconditional love.

To learn more about learning to speak your truth, and listen receptively to the truth of others as well—the shadow behind the "fixes" we offer for issues we can't fix—I recommend Parker J. Palmer's *A Hidden Wholeness: The Journey Toward an Undivided Life*.

NOTES & PERSONAL JOURNAL PAGE

Lesson 7: Laugh Your Way to a Better Marriage

NO SPOUSE IS immune to stress. And one of the best ways to cope with stress is a good laugh. We have all heard about the benefits of laughter for our physical health. It lowers blood pressure and reduces stress hormones. More than that, an increasing number of psychologists who regularly work with couples say that laughter is correlated with relationship satisfaction.

So, laughter is good for your marriage. It relieves tension between individuals in stressful situations. And engaging in humour can help you to see the lighter side of an issue, making most things tolerable. Studies reveal that individuals who have a strong sense of humour are less likely to experience burnout and depression and more likely to enjoy life in general—including their marriage. You need to laugh. So, laugh out loud! It's good for your soul. Take humour seriously.

If you're like most people, you can take life and yourself a little too earnestly, and that always stunts laughter. So, lighten up. Relax. Poke fun at each other. The more you laugh together, the more you love each other. Can you imagine loving anybody with whom you never laugh? Humour bonds you to other laughing souls.

There are, however, a few guidelines when using humour with your partner. Use wisdom and common sense. Don't joke about sensitive issues such as your partner's weight, family, work, and so on. It is critical that the humour not be hurtful or an excuse to get in a jab when you're annoyed. If you are not sure that the other partner will be able to laugh without being offended, it's better to keep the joke to yourself. Sarcasm is one form of humour that needs to be used carefully in relationships, because it can be hurtful if directed at your partner. Same thing with teasing. Be certain that the other person can laugh at themselves in the context of your teasing. Study your spouse and uncover what makes them laugh. After all, each of us has a unique sense of humour. Look for the funny around you, and laugh your way to a better marriage!

NOTES & PERSONAL JOURNAL PAGE

_____

_____

_____

_____

_____

_____

_____

_____

_____

_____

_____

_____

_____

_____

Choose a Winning Attitude
(STEP THREE)

MOST ATHLETES WOULD agree that winning is 90 percent attitude and 10 percent hard work. What we think largely influences what we do. This attitude and action connection opens a door of hope for all couples. Our interpretation of what happens to us (our attitude) is what produces our failures and successes.

Most marriages start off with such a high set point that it's hard for either partner to imagine their relationship derailing. But as John Gottman puts it in his *Seven Principles for Making Marriage Work*, this blissful state typically doesn't last. Over time, irritation, resentment, and anger build to the point that the friendship becomes more and more of an abstraction. Eventually, the members of a couple end up in "negative sentiment override." Everything gets interpreted in an increasingly negative manner. Only a change in attitude will open the door of hope. Step three of The All-*for*-Nothing Marriage Method is to choose a Winning Attitude.

NOTES & PERSONAL JOURNAL PAGE

Lesson 1: Let God Love Through You

GOD COMMANDS ALL people to manifest **agape** love, abundantly, for every-one. When you do, you work for the well-being of others, even if it means sacrificing personal well-being. You cannot do this on your own. You have to die to live this out. I mean to die to your own senses and understanding, and thereby come alive in Christ.

The idea is to be filled with the Maker's vision for that person. To see them in the way that God sees them: precious, valuable, and dearly loved. When you see and hear people as Christ sees and hears them, a gracious love manifests. This sort of love is not talked about enough. God's opinion and perspective trumps all others.

Without divine revelation, people define each other and themselves based on compatibility, shortcomings, physical appearances, what they can produce, what is said about them, and what belongings they possess.

God is the final arbitrator. What you see is not all there is to a person. What you hear is not all there is to hear about a person's story. There is more. Lean not on your own understanding (Solomon, Proverbs 3:5).

Look again, this time through the eyes of your Heavenly Father. You will see clearly. Seeing clearly sets you free. You see people without labels or preju-dices. Compassion begins to seep through you. Suddenly you are transported in prayer, transformed by the revelation. Prayer leads to redemptive action. *Without vision, people diminish people.* The presence of compassion indicates the presence of God. It is impossible to truly love on your own. Only yield to God. Let God love through you. You will not diminish. You will increase.

In agape love, you lose yourself in another's arms, or in another's company, or in suffering for all who suffer, including the ones who inflict suffering upon you. In Christ, to lose yourself in such ways is to find yourself (Jesus, Matthew 10:39). This is what love is all about.

NOTES & PERSONAL JOURNAL PAGE

Lesson 2: Receive the Day

MOST OF US spend the majority of our lives living in an imagined future or imagined past. Because of that tendency, we often experience interactions with others as a means to an end. Rather than experiencing the richness of the present moment, our minds are leaping to the future, filtering each unfolding event as it relates to desires we have for our imagined future.

You might think of it like this: We have two minds. One part of your mind experiences life as it unfolds. The other part of your mind is obsessed with avoiding pain and pursuing pleasure. Being able to anticipate the future is useful, but it should not replace the act of living life itself. Unfortunately, the part of our mind that looks into the future and obsesses about having more pleasure and avoiding all pain can sometimes become too dominant in our thoughts.

Being human means that you will always have a mind-projected future, operating and affecting your emotions. In fact, our ability to look into the future and anticipate events is what makes us so powerful. But living life in the present can be choked out by our desire to control future events. Fear is rooted in our mind-projected future. In the present moment, there is no fear. The present moment is as it is and cannot change, because for anything to change we must add time to the equation. Worry, anxiety, emotional tension, and feelings of stress melt away the more we bring our full attention to experiencing life on a moment-by-moment basis.

The greatest benefits manifest in becoming more focused in the present. Yesterday is gone and tomorrow may never come. All you have is this moment: Today, Jesus says. Do not worry about tomorrow, for the morrow shall take thought for the things of itself. (Jesus, Matthew 6:34)

NOTES & PERSONAL JOURNAL PAGE

Lesson 3: Focus on the Present Moment

ONE OF THE key concepts I have found to be in short supply in cultivating deep and meaningful relationships is the discipline of being present in the moment. In today's society, it is easy to become distracted, fractured into multiple threads of focus so that we are never truly available as a whole to our relationships or interactions. As we become more obsessed with succeeding, or at least surviving, we lose touch with our souls and disappear into our roles. The art of presence is a fundamental concept in Eastern religion, propagated by the likes of Don Miguel Ruiz. But in the Western world, it's a concept that can be difficult to adopt.

In his book, *the Phenomenology of the Human Person*, sociologist Robert Sokolowski describes the use of the phrase "I'm still here" as a "declarative," "existential use" of the term "*I.*" Meaning that using the word *"I"* affirms that one simply exists, outside of purpose or action. He explains, "*When using an existential declarative, I do not promise or dedicate myself to any project in particular; I am just there for whatever may come and whatever needs to be seen or done, but I am still there, and I declare myself as such, as a dative, a person engaged in veracity.*"

Although it may seem subtle, this concept is big, and it helps to illustrate what it means to be 100 percent in. When a person claims "I am here," there is this place of commitment that transcends how you are cognitively dealing with things or votively dealing with things. You are just there. There are at least three benefits to stopping to adopt this mindset that cannot be overlooked and here they are:

First, there is a special, nearly mystic quality to a person who is truly grounded in the present moment. The ability to bring your mind into full contact with the present is a skill that's useful for decreasing anxiety and sustaining vibrant relationships over the long term.

Second, living in the present brings an immense freedom that allows you to experience life rather than judge it or try to manipulate it into becoming something that will serve some desire you have for the future.

Third, when we let go of our obsession with the past and future, life becomes richer and more beautiful. Instead of living in our imagination, we experience life where it's actually happening. This is the day that the Lord has made, we will rejoice and be glad in it.

We can never actually experience life anywhere else than the present. When we rush toward what a relationship could be, we lose touch with our gift, and worse, miss half of what it is now. The relationship is always now. You will never experience the relationship anywhere but in the present moment. Intentionally choose to be present, 100 percent. By letting go of control, a desirable relationship is more likely to emerge. You will feel more confident when doing life with someone becomes a process of spending one moment at a time in the present.

NOTES & PERSONAL JOURNAL PAGE

Lesson 4: Set Aside Every Problem and Focus on Connecting

ALL RELATIONSHIPS HAVE conflict. When problems arise during the day-to-day of our lives, our first impulse is to set out to solve them. However, upward of 80 percent of the problems in most marriages will never be solvable. They are perpetual, forever grounded in the fundamental differences that any two people face.

This concept is one I discovered through my own circumstance. My wife and I are like most people in a cross-cultural marriage. We struggled a lot with how our own stories led us to approach problems in our life together differently. We tried desperately, in our worst spaces, to "solve" our marital problems. But in doing so, we ran away from each other emotionally. The harder my wife and I tried to solve our problems, the more stressed out and defensive we felt. Every time we talked about a problem, not only did we fail to resolve it, we ended up fighting, too.

What we learned through this period is this: If your marriage is stressed, it's not the time to tackle difficult issues. In fact, if the timing is not right, trying to solve problems with your spouse can damage your marriage and make it less likely that you'll ever find resolution. Efforts to make things better will keep making matters worse. Rather than being a source of joy, your marriage will destroy the quality of your life. My wife and I are not the only ones to have had the experience with this truth; others couples reported experiencing the same thing. I liked the alternative approach to counselling.

Our breakthrough came when we started to avoid talking about the issues plaguing our relationship all together (as serious as they were). Instead, we did our very best to focus on *connecting* with each other. We spent the patience and energy we had left building our relationship through practical, positive actions. To our amazement, this was the midnight miracle. Not only did we end up resolving our differences, but we fell in love again! No one told us this would be a redemptive path, the key to a successful marriage. We were just procrastinating solving our marital disputes, exhausted from seeking solutions to them, discussing them, complaining about them, arguing about them. Ultimately, we lucked out. And we did it by maximizing our connection as soulmates while minimizing our obsession to problem-solve.

Mort Fertel says that solving your marital disputes will not create love in your relationship. He was right. I learned this the hard way. Indeed, you might get along better and fight less, but you won't necessarily have a healthy marriage. And your problems will probably reappear or new ones will surface. It's love that solves problems. *Sunlight is the best disinfectant. So is love.* That's the key to a rewarding marriage.

I am with Mort on this: The way to renew your marriage is to take all pressure off your spouse, to temporarily table your issues, and to implement a series of positive relationship disciplines that will strengthen your friendship and create shared meaning. This may seem counterintuitive, but if you strengthen your relationship, most of your problems will dissipate. What remains of them can be more easily addressed in a safer, softer, and more forgiving environment.

NOTES & PERSONAL JOURNAL PAGE

Lesson 5: Take the Pressure Off Your Spouse

WHEN A MARRIAGE turns from sweet to sour, we tend to think it is the other person's fault. That they have changed somehow and that it has ruined everything. But people don't change very much. And it is unlikely that a shift in a person's behaviour has spoiled things. As I said earlier, I am with Mort Fertel on this: Usually it is the loss of *connection* between partners and the associated fading of love that cause the issues. As the old English proverb says, "Faults are thick where love is thin."

When connections become lost, it is often a couple's immediate response to focus on both communication and problem-solving skills. Although these skills may be helpful in some ways, they don't address the heart of the matter, which is the loss of connection. Ultimately, they treat the symptoms but don't touch the root cause. In truth, you could master both communication and problem-solving skills and still be completely unfulfilled in your marriage and without true love in your life.

What is needed is love. Cinderella asks, "Do you love me because I am beautiful, or am I beautiful because you love me?" The answer is B—love is the great beautifier in the universe.

The connection you have with your partner can transform how you experience them. If you're lacking connection, your experience of each other will be negatively impacted. If you reconnect, you will regain the magic of your courtship. You will fall in love again, you will experience euphoric love, and your problems will fade away.

It is love that solves problems, and *not* solving problems that creates love. It is love that creates effective communication, not effective communication that creates love. Love conquers all. It is the root of transformation.

NOTES & PERSONAL JOURNAL PAGE

Lesson 6: Deal with Past Failures

MOST OF US recognize that failure is a reality of life. And at some level, we understand that it actually helps us grow. History's greatest achievers all routinely experienced colossal failures. Thomas Edison reportedly failed ten thousand times while he was inventing the lightbulb. He was quoted as saying, "I have found ten thousand ways something won't work. I am not discouraged, because every wrong attempt discarded is another step forward." The Wright brothers spent years working on failed aircraft prototypes and incorporating their learnings until they finally got it right with a plane that could get airborne and stay there.

Indeed, one can hardly find an historic or current-day success story that isn't also a story of great failure. And if you ask those who have distinguished themselves through their achievements, they will tell you that failure was a critical enabler of their success. It was their motivator. Their teacher. A stepping stone along their path to greatness. The difference between them and the average person is that they didn't give up.

But still, we hate to fail. We fear it, we dread it, and when it happens, we hold onto it. We give it power over our emotions, and sometimes we allow it to dictate our way forward (or backward). Some of us go to great lengths to avoid failure because of all the pain and shame associated with it. We cannot separate these failures from our identities. We cannot stop dwelling on them. We cannot shake off the shame. We all have memorable moments of failure from our childhood that shape or impact what we believe to be true about ourselves, and ultimately, who we become as adults.

Ultimately, we all have to deal with the past before we can put it behind us. Otherwise, it keeps popping back up. Dealing with our past failures begins with sharing our critical scenes with our partners. This discipline can help them to better understand our triggers, those things that make us angry, sad, or even happy. These points are critical to forming connection and understanding one another at the soul level.

Marriage is more than just two people coming together. We get to participate in the healing of each other's stories. Part of that process requires allowing our partners to help reassess our critical scenes and how they might affect our lives together. Past failures can cause us to withhold parts of our true selves and limit our ability to be intimate and vulnerable with the one person we have set in a place with which to be authentic and genuine. If marriage is to be a sacred space where we can be visible and valued, then this process is fundamental and should be embraced. Expressing our past fears with our partners can be redemptive and a necessary step to achieving the meaningful marriage we all seek.

NOTES & PERSONAL JOURNAL PAGE

_____

_____

_____

_____

_____

_____

_____

_____

_____

_____

_____

_____

_____

Lesson 7: Ask a Little Less

IN TODAY'S SOCIETY, we have an increasing trend toward sidelining our friends and relatives while looking to our marriage to help us fulfill our deepest emotional and psychological needs. While doing so, we decrease the invested time and energy allotted for the marriage to meet these requirements. As a result, more marriages fall short of what we need and therefore disappoint us.

What we actually want is a space to become the best version of ourselves. What we end up doing is expecting our partner to be simultaneously responsible for making us feel loved, sexy, and competent, etc. We expect our partners to be our psychologists, financial planners, confidants, providers, pastors, lovers, parents to our kids. We want them to be the best problem-solvers and our sidekicks for every adventure. But in truth, our partners can't be all things. This expectation is too high. Who can fit all of those criteria and still be something unto themselves? These expectations turn us into a burden for our partners, increase anxiety, and cause much suffering.

I would urge couples to consider asking for less, or in other words, to not make an idol of your spouse. Think about what you are looking for from this one relationship and decide: are these expectations realistic in light of who I am, who my partner is, and our dynamics? Ultimately, there is no reason why a single person should play all these roles. We need to examine, realistically, how we can relinquish some of them and outsource them to, say, other members of our social networks.

In general, those that have a larger social network they can turn to for emotional support have an overall higher quality life. By looking to other people to help us, we end up asking less of our partner and reduce the stress and pressure we put on that relationship. There's no shame in thinking of ways that you can ask less. If listed out, I think most people with some experience in marriage would be shocked by how many demands we have piled on top of this one relationship. I'm not saying that people need to neglect their emotional requirements; I'm saying that to get them met properly it's a bad plan to throw all of them on one relationship, trying to do it on the cheap with insufficient time.

Find the places where the demands you're placing on the marriage clearly exceed the amount the marriage can actually meet and outsource them. That's the idea of having a diversified social portfolio.

Psychologist Eli Finkel makes this point very well in his book, *The All-or-Nothing Marriage: How the Best Marriages Work.* If the concepts of asking less and outsourcing are of interest to you and you would like to study them more, I recommend his resource.

NOTES & PERSONAL JOURNAL PAGE

Lesson 8: Develop Wholesome Extramarital Friendships

WE NOW TURN to the issue of isolation in marriage, and the importance of having wholesome extramarital friendships. Developing a social network is healthy and does not diminish marriage, our most sacred relationship.

The idea of embracing an alternative, intimate social network can threaten most contemporary couples. But it needn't. I don't think there's another facet in a relationship that can illicit so much fear, gossip, and fascination. The standard idea is that creating an additional circle of trust outside of your spouse is harmful. That it can lead to affairs, deplete intimacy, or is deceptive, selfish, or cruel.

This concern isn't something to take casually. However, I would argue that **it is not outside relationships that cause marriages to fail apart but a loss of personal connection and directive *inside* the primary relationship. These factors do not dissolve because of outside influence, they dissolve because of inside influence**, specifically through our inaccurate concepts of compatibility, proportionably of contribution (50/50 rather than 100-to-none), and the offering of love, as previously discussed.

Unfortunately, the fear-based concerns contemporary couples have regarding outside relationships influence them toward exclusive love relationships and avoidance of outside social connection. As a result, they may find the experience of marriage isolating.

Most people don't experience significant periods of being socially isolated until after they get married. Before marriage, we tend to be socially active and to interact frequently with our extended family. As a result, the isolating effects of marriage, particularity when children arrive, can catch many people off guard.

Isolation can be very detrimental to one's personal well-being. We often find our purpose in and through our community and typically solve our daily problems through interacting with people who have more wisdom than we do, including parents, siblings, cousins, neighbours, and God. So, when we isolate ourselves from community, we have a higher risk of developing depression and anxiety. This depression and anxiety erode the quality, depth, and prophetic vision that marriage brings to us. They reduce marriage to a hospice where couples nurse this mental illness.

By nurturing those intimate social networks, we build space to free up joy in our marriage. We transfer the ratio of time we spend on problem-solving to quality, intentional interactions. Through this, we can focus on connecting and generating intimacy.

NOTES & PERSONAL JOURNAL PAGE

Lesson 9: Open-Mind Thinking

LEARNING HOW TO both feel and express your emotions is a critical skill for you and your partner to feel safe in your marriage. We are all taught what is appropriate to feel and how to express those feelings throughout childhood, either explicitly or by observation, by our families and friends. As a result, we all have preferences for how to tell (or not tell) our emotions, and are guilty of moralizing these preferences. Sadly, due to fears of being judged or misunderstood by these moralizations, many of us do not feel safe expressing emotions with one another.

Learning to put words to what you feel is necessary for achieving intimacy in relationships—and without intimacy, your marriage will suffer. To support a safe, open space for expression, I recommend what psychologists call "dialectical" or open-mind thinking.

Dialectical means there is always more than one *true* way to see a situation and more than one *true* opinion, idea, thought, or dream. With this way of thinking, two ideas can both be true at the same time: you are right *and* the other person is right. This mindset cultivates a space for freedom of expression that is non-judgmental and filled with the intent to seek understanding. It creates safety for both you and your partner while you learn how to feel and communicate effectively. Here are some guidelines for dialectical thinking:

Firstly, move from "either-or" thinking to "*both-and*" thinking. Couple this with avoiding extreme terms like: always, never, and "you make me." For example, instead of saying "Everyone always treats me unfairly," say, "Sometimes I am treated unfairly *and* at other times I am treated well."

Second, practice looking at *all* points of view and sides of a situation. All people have something unique, different, and worthy to teach us. Sometimes, we have to pause and examine what those might be critically.

Third, find the "kernel of truth" in every side. Remember, *no one* owns the truth. Be open and willing.

Fourth, use "I feel" statements, instead of "You are" statements. Look to assist your partner in understanding your feelings. Actively avoid judgmental statements that shut down communication.

Fifth, accept that different opinions can be legitimate, even if you do not agree with them. "I can see your point of view even though I do not agree with it."

Sixth, don't assume that you know what others are thinking. Check it out: "What did you mean when you said *x?*" Don't expect others to know what you are thinking. Be clear: "What I'm trying to say is *y.* "

If you feel indignant or outraged, you are *not* being dialectical. Being dialectical means letting go of self-righteous indignation, letting go of "black-and-white" and "all-or-nothing" ways of seeing a situation. Seek what is left out of your understanding of a situation. Find a way to validate the other person's point of view and expand your way of seeing things. Get unstuck from standoffs and conflicts, be more flexible and approachable, avoid assumptions and blaming.

By adopting open-mind thinking, you and your partner will experience a connection that is free of fear of judgement, allowing you to reveal your authentic selves. This will truly open the path to becoming effective soulmates.

For more on this, I recommend Linehan, M. M.'s 1993 *Skills Training Manual for Treating Borderline Personality Disorder*, published in New York by Guilford Press.

NOTES & PERSONAL JOURNAL PAGE

Lesson 10: Emotional Sobriety

WE ARE ALL subjected to emotions, those that shape and impact what we believe to be true about ourselves, how we approach life, and ultimately, who we become. Emotions manifest as energies in motion. They are neither good nor bad in themselves. It's what we do with emotions that counts in terms of self-management. Each emotion is a valuable source of information and direction. Urges (even a strong urge) are a natural part of emotions and of being human. However, having an urge does not mean that you have to *do* anything about it.

We are prone to hang onto various lies about emotion, such as: There is a *right way* to feel in every situation. Letting others know that I am feeling bad is a weakness. Being emotional means being out of control. If others don't approve of how I am feeling, I obviously shouldn't feel the way that I do. Other people are the best judge of how I am feeling.

Not only that, we often make decisions based on raw emotions rather than principles. For example, many people are emotionally impaired as a result of various life turns that plagued their life journey. As a result, they have adapted various survival mechanisms (responses) to self-protect and adapt to life. Unfortunately, those responses distort reality and the people in the relationship. Often, a fragmented thought pattern manifests with per-petuation of psychopathological states, exposing deep psycho-social factors, including shame, anger, and fear.

Many people spend all sorts of energy trying to live free of pain. They self-medicate in order to numb their feelings. The key to emotional health is not to deny emotions—the opposite is true. People learn to own their emo-tions so they can manage them rather than let their emotions be in charge. Feelings are the voice of the heart, and you will not have fullness until you're adept at hearing and experiencing all of them. Numbing the dark is numbing the light. Any attempt to block your heart's voice impairs you and creates deep suffering.

NOTES & PERSONAL JOURNAL PAGE

_____

_____

_____

_____

_____

_____

_____

_____

_____

_____

Lesson 11: Five Monster Emotions That Hold You Back

IN MY PASTORAL experiences, mental and emotional injuries are at the root of most relationship breakdowns. Contributing to these injuries, consistently, are dysfunctional responses. I consider dysfunctional responses any attempt at satisfying legitimate needs with illegitimate means. There are five critical relational problems that may thrive on emotional dysfunctions. These are important to identify and address quickly to maintain a healthy relationship with your partner.

First, catastrophizing. For the most part, catastrophizing exposes irrational thoughts that indicate the belief that an occurrence or situation is far worse than it actually is. When catastrophizing, there is a tendency to describe a painful experience in more exaggerated terms than warranted, to ruminate excessively on a specific problem, and/or to feel helpless or hopeless about the experience. Part of these thought patterns can include the irrational and persistent feeling that people are out to get you. Not only that, but people who catastrophize often project catastrophe into the future, forecasting these feelings toward a currently non-existing circumstance.

Second, self and other sabotage. Self-sabotaging behaviours create problems in our lives and interfere with long-standing goals. Among the most common are procrastination, self-medication with drugs or alcohol, comfort eating, and forms of self-injury such as cutting. These behaviours go hand in hand with thoughts like: I don't deserve good things, so I deny myself happiness, opportunities to succeed; I ruin my own success through feeding inappropriate appetites. Sabotage is destructive behaviour that is directed at others as a means to feel powerful, or in control. Sabotaging behaviour can be driven by feelings of jealousy, missing out, or injustice/unfairness. They may also be driven by the intent to not feel alone in our own pain. Sabotaging behaviours can go hand in hand with thoughts like: I don't like what you did to me so I will make sure you don't get what you want—your self-actualization, and your attempt at it.

Third, silent frustration and vindictiveness. These are both expressions of anger, of dysfunctional justice. Vindictiveness can be overt or passive-aggressive, especially in a relationship. Vindictiveness is a strong desire to get back at someone. It occurs when someone feels victimized. This victimization comes with a sense of legitimacy in their attacking behaviour. In these cases, people go after vengeance to, dysfunctionally, bring order to their anger and relieve their pain. However, vindictiveness is deceptive and cannot satisfy. A key indicator of vindictiveness is when people hold grudges and seek revenge.

Fourth, shame. Shame is the motivator behind many forms of broken behaviour. Shame is an intense feeling of angst that makes you wish you could evaporate. It comes with feelings of extreme humiliation and remorse, a despairing of life from abject embarrassment. People often confuse guilt and shame. However, you feel guilt over something you've done and you feel shame about who you are. Guilt is: "I did something bad." Shame is: "I am bad." Guilt is: "I made a mistake." Shame is: "I am a mistake." In psychology, shame is called the "sleeper" emotion, because we are so unaware of its effect in our lives. In the conscious realm, shame produces self-hatred, but in the subconscious, it can produce self-doubt, defiance, rebellion, addictions, withdrawal, or perfectionism, to name just a few.

The difficulty with shame is that it leaves us prone to anger when our natural desires for love, connection, and validation are inhibited by our own ability to accept our self-worth. Shame often manifests as an obstruction to personal growth, spiritual formation, and experience of the fuller Gospel. Toxic shame can undermine being fully present with your spouse and with yourself.

Fifth, absolutism and moralizing. This looks like: My way is the right way; my preferences are normative. Moralizing might be used in an attempt to gain control of a situation/circumstance as a means to rationalize unhealthy interactions. Absolutism can be identified when one places their beliefs above a partner's mental or emotional well-being to win an argument.

When dealing with toxic emotions, try to discern the lies about emotions you're prone to hang onto, for nothing disinfects like sunshine, the sunshine of truth. If you are not a victor over your monster emotions, you will be a victim of them.

NOTES & PERSONAL JOURNAL PAGE

_____

_____

_____

_____

_____

_____

_____

_____

_____

_____

_____

_____

_____

Always Do Your Best
(STEP FOUR)

SO FAR, I have explored the anatomy of marital friendship and furthered our understanding of why it is so critical to relationship success. The positive feelings that engulf happy couples come courtesy of their mutual understanding of each other on a core emotional level: the core connection or attunement. The more highly skilled at achieving it that partners become, the more resilient their friendship and the more solid and promising their future. Some couples are naturals at attunement. But most of us need to work at it somewhat. It is well worth the effort.

The effort to phenomenal marriage begins with Step One of The All-*for-Nothing* Marriage Method, which compels all couples everywhere to *put love first*. The second step is to *tune in to the frequency of your spouse*. Step three is to *choose a winning attitude*. Step four asks each partner in the marriage unit to *always do your best*.

These disciplines are intricately connected to trust and commitment, which form the foundation of a meaningful marriage.

NOTES & PERSONAL JOURNAL PAGE

_____

_____

_____

_____

_____

_____

_____

_____

_____

_____

_____

_____

_____

Lesson 1: Practice the Discipline of Joyful Service

IN THE GOSPELS, Jesus said that "the greatest among you will be your servant." Martin Luther King Jr. reworded it so well: "Everybody can be great … because anybody can serve. You don't have to have a college degree to serve. You don't have to make your subject and verb agree to serve. You only need a heart full of grace. A soul generated by love." Service is a love gift.

Marriage is an intimate environment for serving and modelling the spirit in which to serve. In marriages, serving can often become a burden. It can deplete and end up adding no value. As I said in the chapter called, "Love Gifts that Do More Damage than Good," anyone can easily judge any love gift by the manner in which the gift is given: firstly, joyfully, not begrudgingly; secondly, without expectation; thirdly, with the intent to empower; fourthly, out of what you have; and fifthly, from a healthy versus unhealed place. Serving in a fashion that costs you will lead to exhaustion and bitterness, if you are not careful.

To be effective in service, you need a heart full of grace and joy. The quality of service can be measured by the spirit in which the service is rendered: joyfulness. Joyful service means taking responsibility for yourself and your gift. When you do, the rules of "action-reaction" apply. The redemptive energy you put out will return to you. Joyful service and gratitude perpetuate the same in the universe. The converse is also true. If you notice you are serving begrudgingly, stop. Honour your own integrity: do it joyfully or don't do it at all. Service is a gift that is offered *freely*, irrespective of the worthiness of the recipient. Everyone can be great. To be great is to serve others with great love.

NOTES & PERSONAL JOURNAL PAGE

Lesson 2: Make Decisions Together

THE MOST SUCCESSFUL marriages are those in which husband and wife learn how to function as a team and lean on one another's strengths. Responsibilities are shared according to gifting and ability, not gender stereotypes. If the man is better at planning, he maps out family outings, vacations, and family devotions. If the woman is better at finances, she's in charge of the budget. Each uses their talents and works with the other for the good of the whole. If one tries to do it all, the whole suffers.

When it comes to decision making in a marriage, that is best done together. Studies have shown that the unhappiest people in a marriage are often those who have the burden of making decisions alone. Making decisions should be a shared responsibility. You don't have to decide correctly—you just have to decide together. It's usually better to make the wrong decision together than to make the right decision alone.

So, take the pressure off yourselves. You never know how a decision will turn out anyway. You may think you're right, but it may turn out wrong. You can't control the outcome. So, make your decisions out of peace, not out of anxiety. The best strategy is to decide quickly, as the actual decision-making process should not take that long after you have all the data. Even if you don't actually act on the decision for a while. Spend most of your time managing the consequences of your decisions, not making them.

And trust your Maker. Ultimately, God will redeem all things. Guard your togetherness. Unity is the key indicator to successful decision making in marriage. When you do your best to decide as one, trust that all will be okay, even if things don't work out. If you have love, you can live with any decision. If you're disconnected from each other, nothing will be right any way you look at it. You take responsibility for your unity when deciding things together, and that unity will determine the outcome of your life.

NOTES & PERSONAL JOURNAL PAGE

Lesson 3: Do Your Best to Implement the All-for-Nothing Marriage — 4-Step Plan

FOR ALL OF the concepts described in this book, my request is that you simply **do your best** at implementing them. At face value, doing your best means trying your hardest at something, or putting in your all. But in our performance-driven society, sometimes the concept of someone doing their best can be considered limited, weak, or incomplete. In a desire to promote personal growth, we often push each other to achieve more than what we expect ourselves to be able to accomplish.

But in relationships, when we focus on outcomes rather than someone's earnest intent, it can lead to frustration and failure. In the worst cases, these perceived failures can drive someone initially intent on achieving a goal toward apathy, because they learn—incorrectly—that what they had to give was not good enough.

For the purposes of this book, doing your best has to do with your attitude in doing your part, serving in the context of your marriage. "If you bring forth what is within you, what you bring forth will save you. If you do not bring forth what is within you, what you do not bring forth will destroy you." – Gospel of Thomas.

Your very best is that which is within you. That endowment can enslave or free the world. You may not be what or where you think you ought to be. But you are doing better than you think you are. It is easy to get discouraged when trouble comes, and you are trying to do your best. You may wonder what difference your efforts make. But your best matters more than you think. It may not always seem enough for your partner, but provided you offered the very best of what is within you, that is all that is required.

In marriage, our best changes from moment to moment. Your best is different when you are healthy as opposed to sick. All that is needed is to simply do your best under any circumstance to avoid self-judgment, self-abuse, and regret. In all things, act to your highest level of integrity without expecting a reward. There is peace in the heart of accepting that you have given what you could.

I recommend *The Four Agreements: A Practical Guide to Personal Freedom,* by Don Miguel Ruiz. *The Four Agreements* is an excellent book that discusses comprehensively the topic at hand.

NOTES & PERSONAL JOURNAL PAGE

_____

_____

_____

_____

_____

_____

_____

_____

_____

_____

_____

_____

_____

_____

Why Mom Was Right About Marriage

MY MOTHER DIED very young, before she turned thirty. But from the grave, she still speaks! Although her story has spaces of tragedy, it is one that has always highlighted, to me, the importance of persistence and endurance. My mother lived through two very unpleasant marriage environments. Two marriages to two separate men in two separate countries with the same disappointing result. She married her first husband at a very young age. After she bore her first child, a daughter, her first marriage turned bad. She recalled it as a terrible nightmare and was forced to flee in the night to save her life. Aggrieved over the abortion of her first marriage, she named my stepsister, her first-born, Tabina *Djan wa di*, meaning *Dreams unfulfilled*. Years later, she met and married my dad. As my father's eighth wife, she again did not find the marriage of her dreams, her happily-ever-after moment. Sadly, her second marriage turned into a hostile environment, just like her first. She had her second child, another daughter, and named her *Gnama ni Mina, Di wori tow*, meaning, *All I've got is perseverance*.

My mother realized that the situation from which she had run in her first marriage was exactly the same one she found herself facing in her second marriage. She concluded that running to a third marriage would not solve things for her. So, she dug in and lived as meaningful a life as she could. My mom was considered an honourable lady amongst her peers. She left no inheritance but an anthology of poems, songs of hope and redemption, and jokes and riddles that befit this women with superb humour and gentility of character. She found comfort in creating a library of songs of freedom. She died during the great famines in Boura, Burkina Faso, after a long battle with the effects of polio that deformed her and rendered her blind in one eye.

Although it's easy to focus on the tragic pieces in my mother's story, her message to couples is simple: *persevere, endure.* My mother's life was not perfect. It wasn't the dream she wished it would be, but she chose to endure and persevere, focusing on making the best life she could for herself and

THE ALL-FOR-NOTHING MARRIAGE

her children. My mother's love was one that manifested through persistence and endurance. Her message is summed up in the words of Saint Paul when he said, "Love is patient, love is kind. It does not envy, it does not boast, it is not proud. It does not dishonour others, it is not self-seeking, it is not easily angered, it keeps no record of wrongs. Love does not delight in evil but rejoices with the truth. It always protects, always trusts, always hopes, always perseveres." (Paul, 1 Corinthians 13:4-8)

Without the act of endurance, there is no perfect marriage. The hunt for the perfect home will always turn empty. The hunt for the ideal marriage will always end up in disappointment. But we are called to live to the best of our abilities. To contribute the gift and talents that God has given us. Our relationships do not define that contribution. God gives more grace when the burden grows greater. Just persevere and endure when things are less than you had hoped they would be. There will always be seasons of disappointment in life, but don't give up. There is joy to be found in the journey also.

NOTES & PERSONAL JOURNAL PAGE

_____

_____

_____

_____

_____

_____

_____

_____

_____

_____

_____

_____

_____

CONCLUSION

YOU ARE AT the end of this book but the beginning of The All-for-Nothing Marriage Method for you. This Method only works if you translate what you read into your life. A strong marriage enhances every other area of your life. Creating love is the only way to a fulfilling life.

If you and your spouse become soul mates, you will have everything. If you do not, nothing else will be enough. You could have money, comfort and power, fame, intelligence and beauty…. But If you're not soulmates as a couple, nothing else will be enough.

This was a straightforward do-it-yourself plan to help you achieve a meaningful marriage. To me and my wife, this was a labour of love. Here is a paradigm-shifting approach to recalibrate your expectations, increase intimacy and emotional togetherness, make the most of your relationship, live a better story and experience a meaningful life.

I have brought what lessons the Lord has blessed me with along the journey. I am turning them over to you. You can turn a mediocre marriage into a remarkable one. I am confident that what fruit comes to your relationship, from the steps I guided you through, will be blessed in multitude.

Now that you are armed with the knowledge and the path, it is up to you to get your marriage into shape. And you won't be alone. I'm going to hold your hand and walk you through this process.

The success of your marriage is governed by universal laws of love. I did not invent the universal laws of love. The All-for-Nothing Marriage Method organizes them so you can harness their power in your marriage.

It's not enough to learn about All-for-Nothing Marriage; you need to translate it into action. It is no secret that implementation is a combination of the right consciousness and a discipline that produces results. Inspiration is a lot more common than discipline, so go implement what you've learned now!

For more inspiration, as well as opportunities for other programs including audio, online courses, lectures, life coaching, or how to make peace with God, visit https://www.marriageencounter.ca